TROUT FISHING

TROUT FISHING

BRIAN FURZER

FOREWORD BY BOB CHURCH

WARD LOCK LIMITED · LONDON

© Text Brian Furzer 1988

© Line drawings and artwork
Ward Lock Limited 1988

First published in Great Britain in 1988
by Ward Lock Limited, 8 Clifford Street
London W1X 1RB, an Egmont Company

Designed by Ann Thompson
Text set in 10/11½ pt Times Roman
by Tradespools Ltd., Frome, Somerset
Printed and bound by Rotolito, Milan, Italy

British Library Cataloguing in Publication Data

Furzer, Brian
    Trout fishing.
    1. Salmon & trout. Angling. Manuals
    I. Title

    799.1′755

ISBN 0–7063–6684–0

CONTENTS

Bob Church with a fine brace of stillwater rainbows.

FOREWORD

Trout fishing has been steadily growing in popularity over the last twenty years, throughout Europe, North America, Australia and in other parts of the world as well. The last three years have seen a massive upsurge in the numbers of trout flyfishermen, and there are now more than one million in the UK alone. The fact that the 1988 World Fly Fishing Championships are to be held in Australia is an indication of the universal regard in which the sport is now held.

What is it that has made this great sport take off so dramatically in recent years? There can be no one single reason, but I suspect it is mainly because more and more people are coming to realize just how much flyfishing has to offer. Research shows that many people are passing up the golf course in favour of the lake or river-bank and taking up trout fishing. There can be no doubt that a few days' flyfishing is the ideal tonic for any overworked businessman! The sport is so absorbing that participants forget all their cares as they try to outwit the wily trout, and deal with the many fascinating intricacies of this kind of fishing. There is so much to learn in fishing for trout, and no matter how experienced you are there is always something new and exciting to try out.

For this reason, it is essential to learn the many carefully evolved and specialized techniques of trout flyfishing properly. Only by perfecting your method – through a firm grasp of the basics, a knowledge of some more advanced techniques and a few innovations of your own – can you get the most out of this fascinating and challenging sport.

This new book by master trout-fisherman Brian Furzer will certainly point you in the right direction. Whether you are a novice or an old hand, Brian's comprehensive and knowledgeable text will advance your understanding and increase your enjoyment of the sport. I can vouch for Brian's expertise – he and I have fished together for a long time now, and there is no doubt that he is a very fine flyfisherman indeed. In this book he provides a firm grounding in the basics, and he also lets you into the secrets which have caught him quite a few thousand trout over the years.

Wherever in the world you are fishing for trout, the same golden rules and techniques apply. Success on any expanse of water boils down to locating the fish, be it a river, lake or loch. Then, when you find the fish, what kind of fly and line should you use? There are times when a size 10 Silver Invicta will catch you nothing at all, but a shrewd change to a size 14 of the same pattern will see you net fish after fish. The point to remember on these occasions is that, in a dropping temperature – perhaps after heavy rainfall – the water becomes clearer. This is the time to scale down in size on whatever pattern you feel is right for the conditions.

Brian Furzer's book is full of fascinating and indispensable tips like this, with all the accompanying practical information and direction you will ever need. Whether you are fishing for rainbows with their spectacular dash, or the more sober and cautious brown trout, enjoy your sport. Be kind to the fish, have respect for the environment and follow the sound advice in this excellent book. Do this, and you cannot fail to take pleasure in this great sport.

Bob Church
1988

ACKNOWLEDGMENTS

In my early days I had the good fortune to encounter Bob Church, now one of my greatest friends of long standing, who has helped me and many other trout fishermen who asked him for advice. My thanks to him for contributing the Foreword. Bob introduced me to many other friends; Frank Cutler and the late Dick Shrive are two that freely gave the benefit of their considerable and invaluable experience.

On the writing side I was given my first opportunity by my friend Brian Harris, who (in my opinion) has been succeeded as the best fishing editor in the business by another friend, Sandy Leventon of *Trout and Salmon*.

I would be remiss if I did not mention some fishery owners and managers. My good friend Alan Purnell of Ladybower Reservoir, Derbyshire, introduced me to many excellent days on one of the prettiest waters in England; and David Fleming Jones and Haydn Jones have enhanced my days on Grafham Water. Chris Poupard deserves a mention for the quality of fishing which he strives to maintain at Aveley, Essex, as he did at Bishop's Bowl in Warwickshire. Probably one of the most enjoyable waters that I have fished is Coldingham Loch, near Edinburgh, which is run by one of the most knowledgeable and pleasant owners it has been my pleasure to meet, Dr Eric Wise. My friend Alan Pearson deserves a mention for his dedication to the sport; and my stream fishing was always aided substantially by the cheery approach of Frank and Nigel Wilson of Denford Park at Hungerford, Berkshire.

I must also give thanks to other well-known anglers whose names do not appear in this book, such as Peter Stone, Tom Ivens, John Wilshaw, Chris Dawn, John Buckland and Peter Thompson.

My publishers, Ward Lock, also deserve my thanks, in particular Helen Douglas-Cooper and Len Cacutt for their encouragement.

The most deserving of all is Linda who provides me with such wonderful packed lunches and all the encouragement that anyone could wish for in everything that I take on.

Lastly, I would like to thank everyone with whom I have spent time on the water or at the bar, and to wish them all 'Tight Lines!'

INTRODUCTION

At about the age of ten I started coarse angling, blissfully ignorant at that time about trout fishing. All that I knew of the species came from the fishing publications that I read in my quest to obtain as much knowledge as possible in order to enjoy to the full the wonderful sport that I had discovered.

Some of the local farmers had introduced trout into the streams that ran through their farms and they jealously and energetically guarded these against any poaching from the locals. This led me to the conclusion that trout fishing was just a wealthy man's sport and that I would forever be a coarse angler. However, I was always quite happy fishing on a misty summer's dawn, watching my porcupine quill-tip float and landing many paddle-tailed tench, golden rudd and flashing roach.

It was not until I was in my middle twenties that a friend insisted that I try trout fishing, so I borrowed some of his tackle and accompanied him to a flooded gravel pit, there to catch my first trout on fly, in fact my first trout ever. After more successful trips, I bought my own tackle and the thirst for knowledge was rekindled as trout fishing took over from coarse fishing, and my coarse fishing tackle gathered dust. From that time every spare moment has been occupied with the search for new waters and more experiences with trout.

I discovered that much more trout fishing was available than I had realized. Firstly, there were the large reservoirs; and then, during the 1970s, many small stillwaters burst upon the trout fishing scene. At that time, two distinct factions were created: the small-water flyfisherman, and the larger water (reservoir) angler. The two groups now seem to have merged satisfactorily and many flyfishers start their trout fishing on the small waters and progress to the reservoirs. In fact, the small waters now outnumber the reservoirs and are tailored to suit every pocket, although you should bear in mind that, as with everything else, you get what you pay for. Where they are not stocked with the largest trout, small waters are excellent for novices because they offer quantity rather than quality. It is easier to learn about trout if there are plenty of them to be caught. Whereas a water that stocks particularly large trout may not have as high a density of fish, so the fly is not always in such an effective position. Small waters are also easier to become familiar with; another important requirement in learning about trout.

However, I have to admit that the real love of my life is river or stream fishing, and thankfully this is now reasonably accessible.

It is difficult to define a specimen trout because different waters all have their different characteristics, which influence the growth of the fish. A 4 lb (2 kg) trout from a large water may be of no consequence, but it will be a veritable giant from a stream or loch.

The pressure placed on all waters by the large numbers of anglers has in some areas had unfortunate consequences. However, it would be unfair to criticize fishery owners or managers for exploiting this demand. If a water has been spoilt by over-commercialization, the only protest you can make is to vote with the feet and leave it alone.

Fishing is a social sport, and for this reason I have included some comments on etiquette at and on the water. Hopefully I will not be considered impertinent for doing so, but my own experiences, and those of my friends and acquaintances, give abundant evidence that guidance on this subject will be beneficial to some who have taken up this branch of angling. There are times when we all transgress in a way that could be considered a breach of normal good manners, but I am positive that the majority of occasions are not wilfully meant and are due to lack of watercraft more than selfishness or rudeness.

It will be evident that I continually advocate a confident approach to fishing. I do so because many experiences have taught me beyond doubt

that an angler can catch trout if he is confident of doing so; and conversely, he has no chance of success if he is apprehensive of failure.

This brings me to another matter: trial and error. Many anglers have told me of their ability to remain patient in order to be successful at fishing. However, I suffer from the particular Aries trait of being very impatient, and this, I am sure, points to much of my own success. If I were patient, I would happily fish all day whether or not I met with success. But if I am not successful, my impatience demands that I try every possible technique until success comes. I tell them, too, that fishing is possibly the most tranquil of all sports. At times, everyone must have expressed a real wish that they had never risen from their beds. However, of the many thousands of days that I have spent fishing, there is not one single day when I would have preferred to stay home.

I am not sure that I can define what drives me in my total and consuming dedication to fishing, and I do not recall having heard a satisfactory answer to this question from other anglers. There are many reasons: the nearness of nature, instinct, ego; but it would take a very long time for anyone to tell of all their experiences by the water if they were invited to. Many anglers become attuned to nature to the degree that they are aware of what is happening around them, when they seem to be oblivious to all else but the reaction of the fish. I am happiest on large waters when the day is breezy and the elements are conspicuous; yet I prefer a less windy day when standing in a Scottish salmon river. This is due to the effect of the water as it washes away the pressures of everyday existence among office blocks and traffic fumes. After a few consecutive days' fishing I am fatigued in a glowing sort of way; all the problems and pressures having been purged.

Neither can I offer a clear answer about what it takes to be a successful trout fisherman. The essential ingredient is experience; one must try to catch trout at every possible opportunity and eventually a technique is acquired which will produce the sought-for success.

I have tried as far as possible to pass on much of what I have learnt in trout fishing with a fly; I always consider a day a success if I leave the water with a wet net. For me, total commitment leads to relaxation and enjoyment, and if this book helps others to enjoy their fishing better, then I consider the time spent at the typewriter and my publishers has been worthwhile.

Brian Furzer,
Brentwood, Essex, 1988.

Page 14 *The windbreak created by the trees provides ideal dry-fly conditions on the edge of the ripple.*
Page 15 *The fishing on this type of stillwater is easily affected by the prevalent weather conditions.*

PART ONE

TROUT FISHING ON STILLWATERS

TROUT FISHING
ON STILLWATERS

Today's flyfisherman has a wider range of still-waters available to him than ever before, far more than could have been envisaged when this kind of trout fishing became a business. Available to the angler at that time were large and small stillwaters holding stocks of naturally breeding wild brown trout, but they were soon to be supplemented by the construction of reservoirs, stocked with brown and rainbow trout. More and more enclosed waters appeared from the 1970s on, resulting in a huge expansion of trout fishing.

At that time, there was some fine trout fishing to be enjoyed at British reservoirs in Somerset and Northamptonshire; then Alex Behrendt, recognized as the foremost authority on stillwater trout, turned Two Lakes Fishery, Hampshire,

into a legend. It was the beginning of British stillwater trout fishing as we know it today.

In terms of the trout themselves, it is amazing how breeding systems have turned full circle. The late Sam Holland was the first to use artificial methods to breed huge rainbow trout, fishing for which was made available to all flyfishermen on a day-ticket basis. These trout had been reared by Sam on a high-protein diet until some exceeded

BROOK TROUT Not so popular as it once was in Britain. The brook trout is a char and once acclimatized to a large water, its shoaling instinct disappears, and it fades away in deep, cool water, contributing little to the sport. Its appearance and sporting qualities make it very attractive, and it is unfortunate that it is not suited to large still waters.

RAINBOW TROUT Most rainbows in reservoirs are from the Shasta strain. When first introduced they are heavily spotted and coloured, but their spots largely disappear after they have overwintered.

BROWN TROUT (Reservoir) Popular with anglers, but not fishery managers because of its slow growth. The brown in reservoirs, in perfect condition, takes on a silver livery.

20lb (9kg). He then bred from these large rainbows, creating a new, stronger strain than the original Shasta rainbows from the McCloud River in the area of Mount Shasta, California, USA. These rainbows were first imported into Britain by the late D.F. Leaney in 1932. Then Sam Holland took things a stage further by producing permutations of crosses between rainbow, brown and brook trout, giving the resulting progeny names such as Tiger and Cheetah trout.

These novel cross-breeds enjoyed a short popularity among anglers, then interest waned, as it had done for the brook trout, which is a charr and not a true trout. It was a sign that the original preferences of the flyfisherman for the ordinary brown and rainbow trout had been reinstated, and although many anglers still seek the larger specimen trout which are released into small waters, it is the availability of trout as a sporting fish which outweighs its attraction as a mere trophy.

The prime consideration for the British angler is a fish which will provide the most sport; and this has led to the rearing of the triploid, a sexless rainbow bred from eggs that are treated at the time of fertilization. The result is that these British-bred rainbows do not suffer the high mortality rate this species has so far experienced because they do not respond to their normal breeding season. It was usual to hook rainbows during the autumn and spring when the hens were full of eggs and the cockfish thin and full of milt. In both cases the fish were dark-coloured, provided poor sport and made worse eating. Of course, the triploid treatment does not affect the numbers of rainbows since this species does not breed naturally in British stillwaters, although I have seen small rainbows which could have bred in a feeder-stream leading to several waters. Triploids are not currently stocked in all stillwaters but the successes where they have been introduced should ensure that they do not suffer the fate of the other cross-bred trout varieties. It is too early to know if the triploid will become popular because there are so few, but time will tell.

In contrast, the indigenous brown trout continues to exist as unchanged as the bulldog, and with that lovely animal's same quiet, firm and pugnacious characteristics. I have no hesitation in saying that there is more satisfaction in the capture of a quality brown trout than there is in hooking a rainbow of similar weight, the differences being akin to those between a cart-horse and a thoroughbred.

Regardless of their differences, there is one certain fact: both species complement each other in a well-balanced fishery. It is unfortunate that the brown is slower-growing than the rainbow and therefore not such an economic proposition for fishery owners and managers. But in its natural state the brownie lives longer and reaches a greater weight than the rainbow, so that while flyfishermen are attracted by the thought of the capture of a large brown trout, the free-rising rainbow will provide sport throughout the season. The dour brownie tends to be territorial and feeds deeper in the water unless an abundance of food brings it to the surface, while the rainbow population spreads throughout the water in search of food.

Today, every flyfisherman has quick access to a large reservoir as well as an abundance of small and medium-sized waters, so that where to fish is no longer a foregone conclusion depending on where one lives. The choice now is simple and depends wholly upon the kind of sport one is seeking.

The mobility possible when bank fishing means that, if fish are present in the water, they will, in the end, be located. In the early season the trout will tend to congregate where the wind delivers food and warmer water to them, and they will also be found in the deeper areas that dams provide. It is simply a question of choosing a fishing ground, trying out trusted methods, and waiting for results. If there is no result it is a simple matter of shouldering one's tackle and moving on. If, however, limited success is met with, it is better to persevere in that place, rather than immediately set off in search of more success elsewhere. The reason for this is that if one or two trout are in the area, there are almost certainly more and it could be just a simple matter of fishing at the crucial depth, or speed, or size. Very often, more trout are present than we realize, and the odd take comes from a fish which breaks from the shoal to 'have a go'. This gives the impression that they are few and far between when in fact the remainder are not so daft or hungry as the fish which broke from the rest of the shoal to take the fly.

The essential factor is again confidence, and in the early season this can be sapped by discomfort caused by adverse weather conditions. It is always advisable to overdress than to wear insufficient clothing, because unnecessary sweaters or over-trousers and such can be discarded, whereas they cannot be conjured up from nowhere if it turns out to be very cold. And if, in addition, the results are sporadic, fishing is no joy at all. And this applies equally to boat fishing and bank fishing. I have tried numerous kinds of gloves and mittens and the ones which I consider to be the best are shooting mittens, which have no fingers and thumbs. They consist of a pad that is held to the back of the hand by a thong around the thumb and middle finger and a wrist band. They are just as warm as all other gloves, and have the advantage that there are no fabric fingers that will get wet from handling the wet line, becoming totally ineffective. A long jacket is essential to keep one's back warm, but a shorter one is preferable if deep wading as the water might reach up to the jacket.

All these matters may seem elementary, but it is surprising how often one overlooks a minor item, which can then become an irritant when fishing has commenced, disturbing one's concentration.

ETIQUETTE
It is important to consider how to make sure that other anglers also continue to take pleasure from their fishing.

A fisherman should never intrude on another's territory, thus spoiling his enjoyment. Such be-haviour can be avoided with just a little fore-thought. I have seen situations where this has happened and total ignorance has led to friction and loss of temper.

An example is when an angler catching trout in quite a restricted area suddenly finds others crowding in in such a way that his sport is ruined for the rest of the day. Some anglers lose sight of the fact that others are there for the same escapist purpose. It is simple courtesy to ask another angler who is already in the area if the distance between rods is acceptable.

Then there is the matter of back-casts on public waters. It is virtually impossible to concentrate on one's casting and at the same time be aware of what is happening behind you. Surely, it is the duty of the person passing behind to be aware and to avoid the back-cast if it is likely to be a danger. Of course, where possible the angler should also try to be aware of people passing behind. There is a code of manners in golf and other sports which on some occasions seems sadly to be lacking in fly-fishing. With a little consideration for others our pastime should be a gentle sport *all* of the time.

Because small waters have limited bankspace it is important that fellow anglers should be given special consideration and their sporting chances not be reduced by inconsiderate or selfish action. Anglers can become so engrossed in their fishing that they inadvertently overlook the obvious.

An example of bad behaviour is when an angler has a favourite place on the bank, then wanders off to try another spot, leaving his tackle as claim to the original swim. It is sad to say, however, that this action is often regarded as legitimate and acceptable. On a water where numbers are lim-ited through the size of the fishery, this action is not acceptable. It is the reason why I, and other anglers whom I know, avoid many small waters.

Some fishery owners recognize this problem and impose a time limit on fishing in any one spot, which can be enforced by the angler who chooses to do so. Personally I would not object, for if anyone finds that spot so important I let him get on with it.

Casting into a neighbour's swim is also easy on a small water and is caused by one angler covering a trout moving towards another fisherman. It is often done innocently, but it can cause friction and annoyance.

Small fisheries abound wherever trout are to be found and are an integral part of flyfishing. Some have restrictions on the fishing that render them a specialists' haven, while others have so many trout that they are ideal for learning a great deal about trout behaviour; they are a delight to fish. Every one is different and all are worth a visit. They bear the individual characters of their creators and owners and will test one's flyfishing in one way or another. But remember, the size of the trout is secondary to the enjoyment of catch-ing them.

An angler, wading in order to get away from the rearward bushes, enjoys the solitude of flyfishing on a day likely to produce an evening rise.

BANK FISHING ON STILLWATERS

There are a variety of reasons why many flyfishermen prefer to fish stillwaters from the bank; it may be more convenient, or it may be because a group of anglers prefer to fish together. Of course, the water may have no boat-fishing facility, in which case there is no alternative. It is a fact, too, that there are many occasions when the bank angler will produce more fish than those in boats.

The fact is that stillwater (in the literal sense of the word 'still') does not exist. The agents governing the water's movement are wind and temperature, and the trout react to both factors according to the seasons. Depth is another factor which must be taken into consideration. So, depth, temperature and wind can combine to indicate where the trout may be lying.

In early season, the trout will almost certainly be found in deeper water; if the wind is blowing into a deep corner of the fishery so much the better. Springtime fishing from the bank into a strong wind over deep water will always produce fish. First, the wind blows any edible matter there may be on the surface into a corner and traps it there to form a food source for the fish. Secondly, because the cold weather is on the retreat, the air

temperature is warmer, which in turn raises the temperature of the water's upper layer and the wind pushes this layer into that corner. So the trout will become active in their search for food and congregate in this area – and whenever trout are competing for food they are easier to catch. Thirdly, there will be an undercurrent which takes food and warmer water back into the deeper water.

Tackle selection at these times depends upon the depth of water and the wind strength, and either a floating or a sinking line may be used.

Below *Wind pushes the upper, warmer layers of water into the bank.*

Right *Holding features on a large stillwater: (a) island provides shallows and shelter from weather for fly life, as does wooded bank; (b) shallow bays come into their own as the water warms; (c) deeper water harbours browns and large rainbows during daylight and bright periods: (d) sunken island provides a haven for fry and fly life; (e) dams provide easy access to deep water, and provide uniform depth; (f) drop-off areas always invite cruising fish; (g) sunken hedgerows and roads provide cover from roots, etc., which attract trout.*

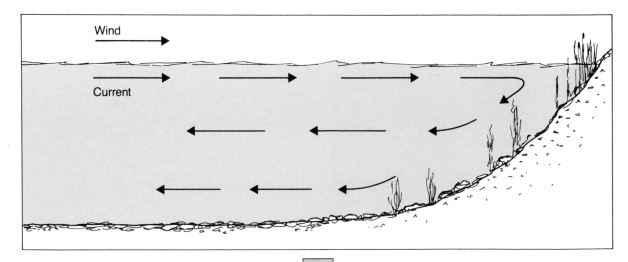

Wind

Current

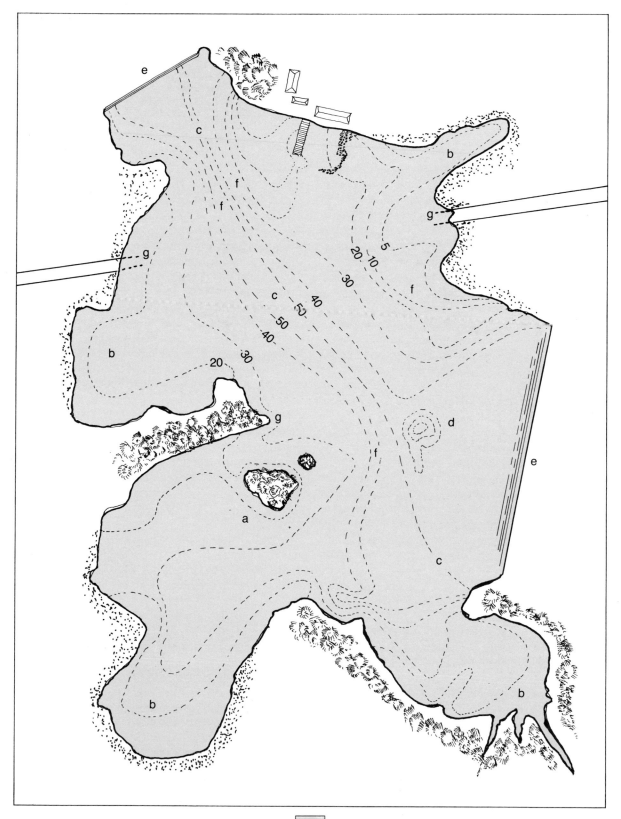

WADING

Wading is necessary at times, but I have never been in favour of it for a number of reasons. First, it does untold damage to plant and insect life in the water-margins, evidence of which can be seen in those barren areas where wading is prevalent. Secondly, I am sure that trout will forage closer into the margins if they are not disturbed by wading anglers. Together, wading and disturbance result in a lack of cover and food, combining to keep the trout well out. This in turn forces flyfishermen to wade farther out to reach the fish, thus exacerbating the problem. Where wading is not allowed, trout can often be seen close to the bank, even in shallow water. Finally, on a matter of personal comfort, I prefer to have all my tackle easily to hand in order that I can cope with fish quickly, either killing them or returning them to the water. These actions are more difficult if one is partly immersed in the water. Fly-casting is also more difficult if the line falls in during the retrieve, unless a line-tray or raft is being used.

Having taken these criticisms of wading into consideration, of course there are places such as wide expanses of shallows or weeds where wading is necessary. However, one should never wade into the water without first reconnoitering the area in case there are fish cruising in the undisturbed shallows. So try a few short casts before wading and creating disturbances that will surely drive any fish away for a while. You might be lucky and take a trout.

If it is necessary to wade, essential items of equipment (apart from waders) are a line-tray or raft, a pocket-sized flybox and a landing-net that is either collapsible or will stick upright into the soft ground nearby. Waders should have a sole which will grip most surfaces, bearing in mind that surbmerged stones are usually slippery. Never buy cheap waders, they do not last long and will probably not have soles that make them safe for wading.

When I have hooked a fish I have always found it convenient to land it from the bank or in very shallow water. To attempt to net the trout while standing up to the thighs in water invites the fighting trout to swim all round you, making things awkward and providing copy for those cartoons we all have seen. So, after hooking a fish, retreat slowly towards the bank and play it as normal. If the water in front of you is shallow it may be difficult to lead the fish into the net, which can put undue pressure on the hookhold and result in the loss of the fish.

A fish should be brought into water just too shallow for it to swim in, this will cause it to cant over onto one side and lose mobility. If you are going to release the trout, do not bother to net it but hold the hook and shake the fish off. It will quickly find its way back into deeper water. Never handle a trout with dry hands if it is to be released. If you are retaining it for the table, despatch it as quickly and humanely as possible. This is important, I have seen trout unhooked, handled, admired, photographed and then killed. Any trout should be killed quickly while it is still in the net.

WADING HINTS
The following points should be born in mind when wading:
□ Remember that 'you get what you pay for'.
□ Loose-fitting waders over insulated socks will best keep the feet warm.
□ Survey the area before entering the water, both for likely holding areas and for safety's sake.
□ Carry a net which will fold and clip to the belt or which will stand in the soft bed.
□ Carry a line tray for storing retrieved line.
□ Try a few casts in the area before entering the water in case fish are cruising or foraging close in.
□ Do not have the water up to the top of your waders on a windy day. The wind will almost certainly push a wave over their tops.

An angler wading on a northern Scottish loch. Here the bottom may be treacherous due to rocks and gulleys.

EARLY-SEASON FLOATING-LINE FLY FISHING

In early season it is almost always necessary to sink the fly well down and to fish it slowly. This means that it is not really practicable to fish straight into a strong wind or even into any wind more than a slight breeze other than with an exceptionally heavy fly. Such a wind would blow a floating line straight back towards the bank with the result that the fly would fish too quickly, added to which the angler would not be properly in contact with it.

At this time of the year the very best position on the bank is to the side of a leeward corner, casting across and allowing the fly to swing round into the corner area. Trout should be caught there. It is all too easy to fish the flies round when in fact the very best tactic is to cast and leave the flies to sink while maintaining contact with the line, letting the wind take it round in an arc so that the flies end up among the trout, moving at the same speed as everything else on the water's surface and being driven in a natural fashion before the wind.

It is essential to be ready for any movement of the line because one must not retrieve until the flies have fished out a cast on their own. One must keep a responsive touch to any increase in pressure on the line because a trout can pick up a fly, reject it and be long gone before our comparatively slow reflexes can react, and for this reason absolute alertness is essential.

Flyfishermen will talk of a 'smash take', but in fact it does not exist. Certainly, trout may take a fly at speed, but what probably happens in over 90 per cent of these cases is that the trout picks up the fly and either it feels the hook and bolts, rapidly tightening the line, or, because the angler is retrieving at the moment the fish bolts, he pricks the fish or sets the hook, producing the same effect. In any of these cases a 'smash take' can result if the angler is not alert. The result is that the fish swims off with the fly or team of flies, plus monofilament, all hampering its movements and threatening its life. This is bad fishing, not

desirable and easily avoided with a little thought.

In this situation, losing a fish can be avoided by maintaining concentration on the farthest point of the fly line and by *not* clamping it firmly to the rod while the line is in motion, either because of wave or wind action or due to the line being retrieved. Any deviation in the course of the line will be seen and a strike should instantly be made, resulting – hopefully – in that tightening of the line as it is picked up from the surface and the rod bends to the bucking of the trout. Alternatively, one can watch the slack where the line leaves the rod tip-ring and falls to the water. This 'corner', formed as the line reaches the water, will straighten out as a fish takes the fly. For obvious reasons, the motion is not as instant an indication as any movement of the farthest point of the line will be. If a trout has taken the fly as the line is being retrieved the line will not fall back onto the surface between pulls, and so the next pull should produce a firm tug back from the fish and the strike should be made immediately.

In all cases, if the flyfisherman is not heavy-handed or clumsy, the line should not break as the fish takes and the strike is made. When clamping the line to the rod-butt it must be remembered that consideration must be given to the breaking-strain of the leader, and the finger responsible for tightening the line should only be allowed to act as a clutch, giving line in response to a heavy pull from the fish. It must be emphasized that it is unwise to use a light breaking-strain leader with a large fly, because there is insufficient line strength to set the point of a large hook beyond the barb, where one is used.

Right When a fish takes the fly with the line at (a), the line at the rod tip will straighten (b). The strike should be made immediately.

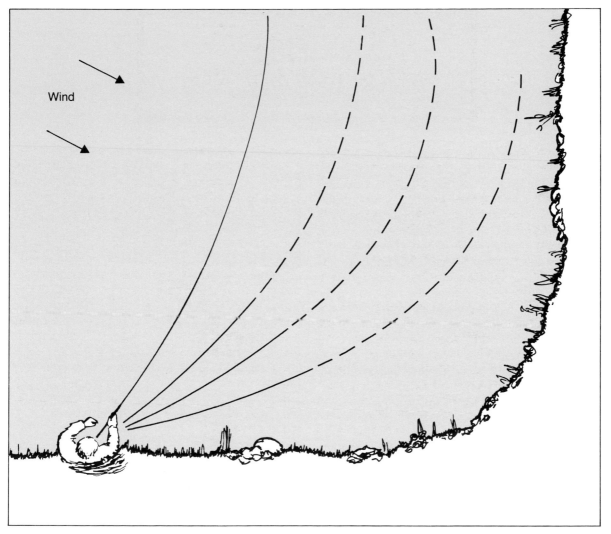

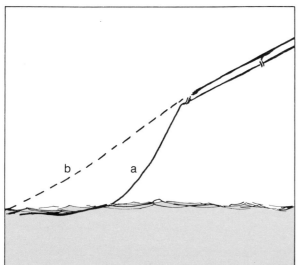

Above *When casting across the wind and holding the line firmly, wind action will push the line into the corner. Casts made to different lengths will cover the corner efficiently.*

AS THE WATER WARMS

Fly life is limited in the early part of the season. The majority of insects which are about are known as buzzers and there are plenty of caddis larvae too which fall prey to trout as they forage deeper. At this time of the year almost any colour and/or size of fly will take fish so long as it is fished in the right place and at the right time. Later in the year, however, the food supply becomes more plentiful as the water warms, causing the trout to spread out and roam the water. They can become 'educated' too, and this is the time when the angler must be aware of the likely movements and feeding habits of the trout.

I have proved to my own satisfaction that the fish become conditioned to which flies are harmful to them, obviously because they may have been hooked and then broken free on a particular fly pattern. That pattern then becomes connected with alarm and danger, these reactions being associated with either the colour or the movement of the fly. In the early season, I have been systematically catching trout in one particular spot when they have suddenly gone off and I have failed to find one even when fishing at different depths and with varying speeds of retrieve. However, a change of fly pattern and the sport has returned to its previous level. If a fish is hooked and lost twice in succession, another change of fly is necessary. I have also seen trout in clear water reacting to a recognized pattern, suggesting that the fish has been hooked and lost, or pricked, before on that fly. This is the major reason why I try to include an element of difference in all the fly patterns that I tie myself, for as the season progresses I have found it pays to assume that every trout in the water becomes much 'wiser', particularly with regard to bank-fishing anglers. Later in the year, one must fish very cautiously and use imitations as close to the natural food as possible. The only exception to this may be when cooler weather arrives later in the year; now, the trout throw caution to the wind as they move into the margins and shallows to chase small fry.

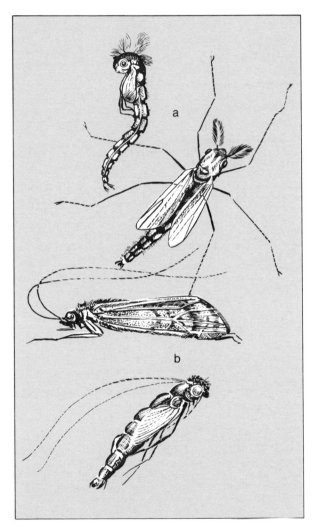

Two different, but very major, items of fly life that are common in trout fishing:
(a) the sedge fly adult and pupa;
(b) the Chronomid *('midge' or 'buzzer') and pupa.*

Right *Casting to a rising fish on a small stillwater, Leominstead in Hampshire, England.*

30

MID-SEASON TROUT FISHING

To be successful in trout fishing, it is of paramount importance that anglers understand some of the reactions of the fish in terms of habits and habitat, and this is where brown and rainbow trout can vary enormously.

The rainbow tends to roam freely over its waters, while in general the brown trout is much more territorial, gravitating towards one particular area and staying in the vicinity until its natural spawning instincts drive it away as the water cools. Usually these areas are places where the bottom of the lake or reservoir abruptly changes from sloping to shelving, the larger browns tending to stay in deeper water and moving about only during quiet or dark periods.

Whatever I say about trout behaviour must be qualified, for the words 'never' or 'always' do not apply. There are always a few fish that defy logic and there are many occasions when the normal behavioural pattern does not happen, and here a long shot can pay off. I have had many good days trout fishing which, try as I might, I have been unable to repeat and for no obvious reason. This is what makes trout fishing so compulsive for me. All that we can hope to do is learn enough on those occasions to enable us to enjoy the sport more and to help others do the same. Generalizing about trout would be easier than trying to classify browns and rainbows in terms of bank fishing, and in any event browns can always turn up among a bag of rainbows.

Wind conditions are always as massive an influencing factor in warmer weather as they are in the early season. There is a difference in that fly life is more inclined to hatch in warm water, making more food available to the trout. The fish is cold-blooded, which means that warm water increases its metabolism, giving it the energy it needs to swim in search of food. This sustenance is needed to replace the energy used, and so a natural, logical cycle is created. All trout eat insects, which means that these creatures are of prime importance as part of the trout's food chain.

Brown trout particularly will hug the bottom in deep water, and where there is a steep drop-off fish will be present.

Water movement takes insects about and usually trout will swim up-wind, taking food as it is carried along on the wave action at the surface. On days when there is a ripple on the water the best fishing position is one that enables the angler to cast comfortably across the wind, and better still if a point is available which protrudes into the lake. Unless you are fishing in deep water from a dam wall a floating line or one of neutral density should be all that is needed in mid-season.

The depth at which the fly is fished is absolutely crucial in mid-season. It is so important that merely the length of the leader can make the difference between a basket of fish and a dry landing-net. Of equal importance too is the size and weight of the fly being used.

The first thing to consider is the size of the fly to be selected. A careful look at the water and margins may reveal something that makes your choice easier. Feeding fish are the next thing to watch for and this may not be easy from the bank, but time spent scanning the water is never wasted. Should a good, healthy, swirly rise be seen then the trout are moving to the surface. A flat spot in the waves indicates that a fish has turned just below and has just taken a nymph or fly struggling in the surface film.

The pattern of fly one selects is a matter of personal preference, and it is a fact that some flyfishermen are unable to catch fish on a certain pattern while nearby another angler might be catching fish regularly on that same artificial. One of the ways to narrow the odds is to use more than one fly on the cast and in favourable conditions even four flies could be an advantage, giving variation in pattern, colour, depth and style. Of course, this is only possible if the fishery allows more than one fly on the cast.

It is not suggested that more than one fly should be fished as a matter of course, but there are occasions when a team of flies is a distinct advantage because:
□ More than one fly in a group might attract the attention of a fish which would otherwise be disinterested.
□ It is spreading the load in that more than one pattern is being presented to the fish.
□ If a trout comes to one fly and rejects it, it may still take another one on the cast.
Then there are the disadvantages:
□ There are obvious casting difficulties.
□ The leader will be weighted with more than one fly and might fish below the required level on a slow retrieve.
□ If a fish does come to one fly on the cast the presence of others moving in unison might alarm it. This is a strong possibility with 'educated' fish.
□ Although one fly on the cast might appear natural, the retrieve may look unnatural for another fly on the same cast. This implies that great care must be taken on the cast.
□ A second trout might take a trailing dropper

Fishing from a protruding point on the bank. A floating line will progress during the retrieve from positions (a) to (c).

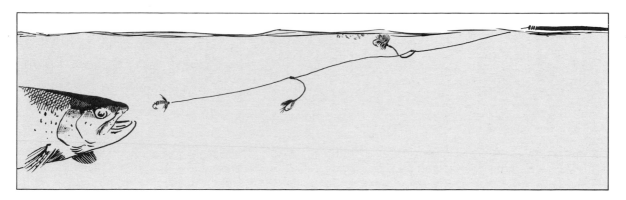

If the flies are allowed to settle before the retrieve begins, they will fish at the correct level throughout.

while the angler is playing a fish to another fly on the cast. He might land two fish – but he might also lose one or both.

□ The dropper might foul weeds or some other obstruction while a hooked fish is being played, resulting in lost fish or broken leader.

My preference is to use three nymphs or wet flies, using a blood-knot to attach the dropper rather than a four- or five-turn water-knot. I am happier fishing a cast which has droppers tied with blood-knots and if I feel happier I fish better, something that every angler knows. However, some flyfishermen would never consider a blood-knot and they catch fish: the sport is all about relaxation, so it is important that we all fish in whichever way we are happiest.

There is one knot about which I am adamant and that is the turl, which I use to tie the flies to the cast. My reason for this is that first and foremost there is nothing showing forward of the fly. Secondly, the fly will not 'hinge' itself round the turl-knot as it does with the half-blood, but has to follow the pull of the line at an even keel, swimming more naturally. The third reason for preferring the turl-knot is that it is round the head of the fly and can hold in a loose dressing. This is a boon when a favourite fly is the last one in the box and falling apart through constant use. A useful hint when you are using a turl-knot at the end of the day is to make sure you take the knot off the fly while the line is still wet. It is difficult to change flies in haste if a dry remnant of a turl-knot is clinging to the artificial.

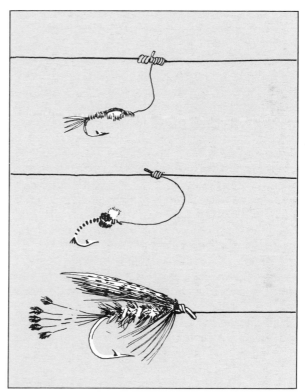

Top *Blood knot dropper.*
Middle *Four-turn water knot dropper.*
Bottom *Flies tied to the leader with a turl knot do not 'hinge' on the leader, and show no knot to the front of the fly.*

Opposite *The pleasure of hooking and landing a fish amid these surroundings must have been very satisfying for this fisherman as he brought his prize to the waiting net. The trees shelter the area, thereby encouraging insect life and attracting fish.*

NYMPH FISHING

If trout are not feeding at the surface it is fairly safe to assume that the fish, unseen, are feeding below. I believe that there are always trout feeding deep at any time, even when they can be seen rising all about. Another assumption that has to be made, is that trout are actually occupying the area you have chosen to fish. The next factor to take into consideration is at what depth the fish will be feeding, near the surface or deep down, and it is here that a knowledge of the actual depth of water at the farthest point of a retrieve will be more than helpful and is essential. A good depth of water to fish in mid-season is about 8ft (2.5m).

If your cast is to fish within the first few inches of the surface, either a single fly or multiple 'light' flies are necessary. Here, 'light' does not mean that the flies have to be small or lightly dressed. The first consideration is a lightweight hook, for the fly can be bulky as long as the materials are not heavy. For instance, seal's fur and deer hair will aid buoyancy, as will hair or fur of most kinds. A fly that is thinly dressed on a heavy hook will cut through the water well and sink quite rapidly. Fish see and are attracted by a sinking fly, so if trout are thought to be near the surface the artificial must sink slowly and naturally to them.

Trout that are worth catching in mid-season are more wary and so imitative fishing is by far the best way to take them, unlike early-season trout which, having not been long in the fishery, will eagerly take a fly of any size and colour at any speed. In put-and-take fisheries there are recently-introduced trout that will respond to most things that move anywhere near them but they are usually never specimens or trophy fish except on a small water.

The types of fly to use in mid-season are those with a natural appearance, such as Pheasant-tail Nymphs, Stick Fly, Hare's Ear Nymph, Buzzers of various colours, Sedge Pupae, Bloodworms, and so on. The choice is limitless but it will quickly be narrowed down through experience.

I recall fishing the 'No Wading' area at a large English reservoir on a warm and windless day. There were numerous anglers in the vicinity and I found that the trout were very difficult to catch, as did everyone else except one angler who had taken half-a-dozen fish, as many as all the other fishermen combined. Eventually I swallowed my pride and asked him why he was doing so well while the rest of us were failing. It turned out that he was a regular visitor to the water and so knew it well, and secondly, he was full of confidence that he was in the right place and fishing correctly. Then he gave me a fly matching the one he was using. It was an expertly tied Bloodworm, Size 16, with a tiny blob of lead at the head, painted red, and had a red-ribbed body with a stub of red maribou for the tail. As I talked to him, he caught one more fish and missed another, casting the fly and leaving it to sink, the maribou tail giving it life. Sometimes a trout would take it on the way down, and if not he had the confidence to let it sink to the bottom, leaving it there to be picked up by yet another trout. This to me was a classic combination of knowledge, competence and confidence. I was catching the odd trout and so were the others but this young man was beating us all.

On the subject of fishing the static fly, remember that some fisheries do not allow it. It lends itself to being abused by the unscrupulous minority who use bait and ruin the sport for those of us who play the game. 'Static' fly does not include the dry fly in its definition, only the sunk fly. On its day and when used correctly and at the right time the static fly method can be deadly and most waters will respond by producing trout.

Once you have decided where to fish and with which flies, the technique is a matter of educated trial and error. It is also important that you keep a watchful eye on what is happening in your vicinity so that if the trout start to rise, or cease rising, you can change your method accordingly. If there is evidence of fish rising one should present nymphs near the surface. Select small flies and grease the leader, causing the flies to work in the surface film or just beneath it. If there is a ripple coming from one side and there are trout moving in the ripple towards your flies, providing they are the correct patterns catching trout should be an academic exercise.

The fact is that these conditions occur with reasonable frequency but thankfully the trout do not cooperate in a suicidal manner. This means that the angler has to take stock, sit down and think the situation through, not an easy thing when there are fish rising about you and you are aware that at any moment they may pass on or cease rising. But to flog away without results produces nothing except frustration and a head empty of knowledge. The thing you must do is wonder why the fish are not taking your fly. Could it be the depth you are fishing? The colour? Is the leader or the fly line showing, or some other factor unseen by you but visible to the trout – and there are plenty about!

So, if the fish persist in rising around the fly and continue to ignore it, the answer usually is that your fly does not match the insect upon which they are feeding. It also may mean that your fly is fishing too deep, or that other flies on the cast are making the trout wary. This can be remedied either by removing all but one or replacing the other flies on the cast with a pattern that is currently preferred. If your size and/or depth are wrong, only trial and error will show the correct fly. I have found that it is best to remove all but one fly and when I have had a result with it I consider whether or not to fish with more than one.

The retrieve can be all-important. With a ripple coming from the side a static or very slow retrieved fly should produce results, but there will be occasions when a stripped nymph, retrieved rapidly, will quite inexplicably take a fish. I attribute this to the natural aggression of the trout being aroused by a rapidly moving item of 'food' and forcing it to take. Another factor to take into consideration is that due to the rate of retrieve the fish is not afforded an opportunity of a detailed examination as it would be if the retrieve were slow.

To continue discussing the reasons for fish not taking, if you find that fish are being cast to, and covered, and are still ignoring the fly but rising again then all is well with your presentation: it is the fly that is at fault. However, if the trout rise regularly on their approach, are covered and then stop rising or shows signs of alarm, all is not well with your presentation. It may be a badly timed or badly presented cast – and you will know it. If the presentation is natural and still the fish are alarmed sufficiently to stop rising they must be aware of the angler either by his silhouette or by a poor knot or a flashy fly line. Sometimes a highly varnished rod will keep the fish well out of casting range of the angler, but usually it is a poor cast or the leader that will alert the trout.

On many occasions I have fished alongside anglers from a bank and, particularly on waters where there is a damwall, I have found that with numbers of anglers fishing close together the fish often decline to run the gauntlet of innumerable lines and flies, and rise only beyond the average

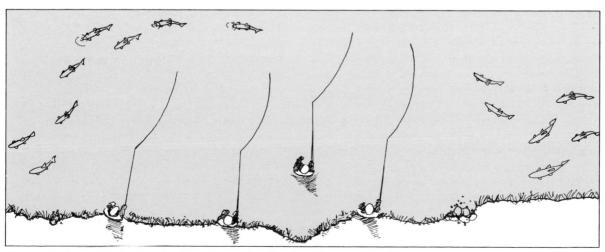

Trout will give a wide berth to bank activity, rather than 'run the gauntlet' of lines.

The wide open reaches of Australia surround this angler.

Australian brown trout is the progeny of original British fish, stocked by Captain Hamilton.

The main ingredients of a trout's underwater diet: (a) small fry; (b) corixae; (c) damselfly nymphs; (d) chironomid ('midge') pupae; (e) sedge pupae; (f) emerging sedge; (g) adult sedge; (h) mayfly nymph; (i) adult mayfly; (j) daphnia; (k) freshwater shrimps; (l) caddis larvae; (m) chironomid larvae (bloodworms).

casting distance. In these circumstances I have taken fish either by casting slightly farther than the average angler, or by moving away from the line of anglers. This is where correctly balanced tackle is imperative, for one can strain a rod by trying to make it cast too far with a line not matched to it.

Try to project your imagination down the line and see things from the trout's point of view. Where there are many lines, some sinking, some floating, with singles or teams of flies all creating shadows and disturbances, any fish will be kept away, except the stock-fish. Older and 'wiser' trout will give the area a wide berth, but they still have to feed and so can be taken if you give the matter some thought. Thinking like a trout (even

though fish cannot 'think', but you know what I mean) has often been an invaluable aid to me.

There was one balmy summer's day when Brian Harris and I were fishing Farmoor 1; the trout were rising freely but ignoring all offers. Brian is the best nymph angler I know, so the fact that he was not catching fish meant that some hard thinking had to be done. Ladybirds were the only natural food source in evidence but we both could not believe that the trout were preoccupied with those insects. I sifted through my flybox, finding nothing that resembled a ladybird, so I opted for a Claret Nymph tied in shellback fashion. In no way did it resemble a ladybird but the size and shape were about right, and it solved the problem, for the first trout I covered took the nymph and when we examined its stomach contents we found it full of ladybirds.

We both used this fly pattern and caught trout but the triumph was short lived because the fish 'went down' soon after. Since then the 'silhouette' method has worked for me on many occasions,

the claret-nymph-cum-ladybird bringing many trout to my landing-net.

It pays to be constantly thinking about how the trout are behaving, how your fly is fishing, what other anglers are doing, and so on. It is also essential to be versatile at a moment's notice, even if at the time it doesn't seem to be logical. Very often there are factors which influence the trout's behaviour which we do not recognize, and this is where a regular companion proves that two heads are better than one.

I recall an evening at Grafham Water when Bob Church and I were covering rising fish regularly without reward, for we did not know what the trout were taking. We greased our leaders and tried all sorts of things and I eventually tied on a small corixa imitation, greased the line again and cast across the wind. Success was immediate and constant, every fish I covered – and some I hadn't seen – took the fly, so I gave a fly of the same size and tying to Bob, but he still had no luck.

When I said 'I suppose you greased the leader right up?' it produced an explosion from Bob, who good-naturedly asked why I hadn't told him that, for we both knew immediately what the difference was – next to nothing in terms of fishing depth of the fly because it was an unweighted seal's fur pattern. But with a degree of forethought and, admittedly, luck I had hit on the right permutation. Luck is that magic ingredient that we all need from time to time.

In my opinion a good nymph fisherman is possibly the angler for whom I have the most admiration. He must rely on presentation and imitation, for there are always fish feeding on underwater food but finding the correct size and presenting it at the right depth are matters as equally important as the actual imitation. The nymph flyfisherman is not relying upon the retrieve or a garish splash of colour incorporated in a fly to deceive his quarry, he relies more on his knowledge of the water and his experience to track down and hook his trout.

41

FISHING A DRY FLY

The object of dry-fly fishing is to deceive the trout into rising to a floating imitation of an insect, so providing that classic sport which we all dream about while sitting by the winter fireside.

Trout will take the dry fly at any time and under any conditions, providing it is fished long enough but there are times when it is more successful than others. On a cold, blustery day the dry fly might not be selected, but during a mild day or evening, when the fish can be seen rising splashily to olives, sedges or any other fly which is hatching at the time, the dry fly must be considered first.

The dry fly is of great importance to the river fisherman, but it must never be discounted by the reservoir angler and there is never a time when it should not work when the trout are feeding on top or cruising somewhere just beneath the surface. Conditions will be better on some occasions than on others, but if the fish are inclined to rise but are not responding to other methods with any regularity, then the dry fly could be the answer. It should always be considered on those madly frustrating evenings when the trout are rising to a prolific hatch (usually the tiny caenis) and are refusing all the angler's offerings.

Then, a tiny Grey Duster or other imitation will be cast out and left among the cruising trout, and sooner or later there is a result, the main reason being that on these occasions there is little or no wind and the trout are 'smutting' – lazily cruising and picking spent flies off the surface film. A wake is created by the leader if you fish a fly which has to be moved to keep it high in the water and this gives the fish ample warning that the fly must be avoided. In contrast, if a dry fly is cast out and left to float in the film, as the naturals are doing, fish may well take in the imitation without first inspecting it.

In order to avoid the fly being inspected by a wary trout it is essential that the leader to the fly must be sinking. A leader floating on the surface is nothing more than an arrow pointing to the imitation and trout will give it a wide berth.

Another necessity is that once the fly has been positioned it is not pulled into the path of the cruising trout as they approach it. The fact that the fly is on the surface and the leader – hopefully – is sunk, eventually means that one of two things will happen, either the leader sinks the fly or the fly floats the leader, neither of which is desirable or effective. The way to cover a rising trout is to lift off the dry fly and cast it so that it lands in the path of the fish.

If the leader has been properly treated it will sink immediately, and here I have found that a leader rubbed with ordinary waterside mud will lose much of its glint and grease and will sink. But a word of warning – every time the leader is handled it will acquire grease from the hands and must be treated again. Sometimes, a dry fly which is sunk and is being retrieved quickly will be savagely seized by a passing trout, but do not rely on this as a reliable method. The best way to fish a dry fly is static, keeping in touch just sufficiently so that when a fish takes the strike can be effective.

The question of when to strike is one that causes much frustration, but in the long run the best method to use is the one that works for you.

Above *A sunk leader will be less obvious.*

Right *A good catch of double-figure rainbows.*

We have all heard about phrases which must be mystically uttered before tightening on a fish, but if the fish is moving quickly it will have the fly effectively in much less time than will a trout that is lazing along. There is one certain fact: the fish will not be firmly hooked if it has not been allowed proper time to get its head back down to the natural swimming position. If it rises, takes the fly and is then struck while 'looking up', the hook will not and cannot pull into a secure hold. All that will happen is that the fish will be hooked forward through the mouth, possibly by a piece of skin which gives way immediately, usually resulting in a lost trout.

On stillwaters, dry-fly fishing is not as much of an art as it is on rivers and streams, but it definitely has its place in the armoury of the stillwater troutman and should always be considered even if it merely provides respite from hard fishing on an unproductive day or perhaps fills in time during the dog period between daytime activity and the evening rise.

The type of dry pattern that is successful depends largely on the water and only experience and observation will supply the answer – as will the fish. The most popular patterns are the sedge family but many others are effective and I will not discuss the complete range. However, it seems that there is a return to the traditional patterns and that flyfishermen have to a large degree given up the constant experimentation that seemed to prevail for a time and are now fishing those old and faithful flies which have caught so many trout

over the years. Fly tyers still experiment of course and sometimes meet with great success but few of their pattern ideas make an impression on the sport in the way that, say, the Lake Olive or Tup's Indispensible did, and until they have had the same success they will not.

The dry flies I use are the bi-visible Sedge, Tup's Indispensible, Grey Duster, dry Hare's Ear, Up-winged Olive, Daddy-Long-Legs (Crane Fly), and various other sedge and olive patterns in both palmered, up-winged and spent tyings. There are few situations that cannot be covered by a sensible spread of dry fly patterns, and size is usually more important than any other factor. Get the size and colour right and success will not be far away.

In recent years dapping has become popular on stillwaters at certain times of the year, especially when the daddy-long-legs (or crane-fly) is blown onto the water in late summer. Some waters will allow the natural daddy-long-legs to be used, but most insist that artificials are sufficient. The object is the same as in dry-fly fishing in that the fly is kept afloat, but it skips onto and off the waves in the way that an insect would do if it were laying eggs or struggling to take off again.

Dapping is more often carried out from a boat, but it can be done from the bank with the proviso that there must be a healthy following breeze and there must be fish within very easy reach because no casting is done.

The essentials are a long rod – as long as possible – in order that the fly can be kept aloft

The strike: if made at (c), the fly will be pulled away from the fish. The strike should be made at (d).

and some floss blow-line, which most tackle dealers stock, in lieu of the normal casting line.

A length of floss line is attached to a monofilament backing of only about 10 lb (4·5 kg) breaking strain; the floss line being about 5–8 yd (4·5–7·5 m) in length. The aim is to achieve a set of light tackle which will be blown by the wind well out in front of the angler, the floss line acting as a sail. A length of cast is then attached to the floss line, to which is attached a well oiled artificial or a bunch of natural insects. The angler holds aloft the long rod until the wind takes the floss, at which time the flies can be released to be carried forward. More line can be released as required. The flies are then dapped onto the surface without any of the cast touching the surface if possible. The wind will inevitably lift the flies from the surface, and it is a simple matter to return them to the surface by lowering the rod or releasing more line.

When the trout takes a dapped fly it can do so in a number of ways. Dapping also accounts for many large trout, so it is as well to be prepared. Often the trout erupts from beneath the fly in a similar fashion to a guided sea-to-air missile, taking the fly either on the way up, or on its 're-entry'. Sometimes there will simply be a sudden swirl and the fly disappears. In every case, it is essential that the rod tip is lowered to give the fish some line. Then, as you see the leader moving away, is the time to strike. Whether the fish is hooked or not, this is probably the method that pumps one's adrenalin harder than any other. It is

important that at all times the floss blow-line is kept dry while it is in the air. If it becomes waterlogged, it will not be carried on the wind.

Another 'dry-fly' technique which has gained in popularity in recent years on stillwaters is the floating fry. This is an imitation of a dead or wounded fry floating on the surface and is very successful at the back-end of the season when trout are feeding on fry in the margins.

The fly is usually made of spun deer hair along the length of a long-shank hook about size 8 or 10, which is then clipped to the shape of a small fry and painted, if wanted, to match a small perch in colour. It is cast near to weed beds and left to float in the surface film. The fry-feeding trout usually swirls at the fly and takes it, and the strike should be just as when fishing with any dry fly.

Fry feeders in the margins will usually be betrayed by small fry leaping from the water, and by the occasional swirl as a trout smashes into a shoal of fry and turns in their midst. The floating fry is intended to represent a helpless casualty of these forays and to induce the trout to take it, as he would expect to find such a casualty in any event. It may be necessary to give just an occasional twitch to the fly to attract the attention of the trout, but usually, on stillwaters, the fly will eventually take a trout if it is fished with sufficient persistency.

FISHING A WAKE FLY

A wake fly, as its name implies, creates a wake on the surface. It may be fished as the top dropper on a team or as the only fly on the cast. This fly deserves a mention because it can sometimes be very deadly, but there is one qualification and that is that it can also be a complete failure. Give it a try when fish are not moving or if they are totally ignoring all other offerings. But if you try the wake fly for ten minutes without results, it will not be worth pursuing.

Any buoyant fly may be tried but a Muddler Minnow of the correct size is one that can also be very successful. At dusk, the classic imitation is the White Moth and the best time to cast it is in failing light, when the surface is either flat calm or close to it. Now, the fish have finished the evening rise and gone down, but the odd one, sometimes a very big trout – can still be tempted to the surface. The light needs to be quite poor.

On one occasion I rose a number of fish on a bright, brassy day when the water was flat calm. I was fishing a Size 14 Muddler Minnow very slowly over about 10ft (3m) of water. There were several trout in the 2lb (1kg) region, with the best fish that came up to the fly looking to be a brown trout of 6 or 7lb (2.7–3kg) but unfortunately the hook failed to hold.

It is vital that the leader should not be visible to the trout, and it can happen mostly when there is a ripple on the surface or the light is dim. Remarkably, the ripple produces another anomaly, for I have found that sometimes the trout will only take the fly if it is pulled up-wind, against the ripple, and on other occasions fish will take only if the fly is retrieved across the ripple. I have never understood why but it must be something to do with refraction. So it is always worth bringing a fly down as well as across the wind for a trial period.

The retrieve is of crucial importance. Most effective is the steady figure-of-eight method, although at times a very fast strip works better. Sometimes a fish can be tempted by simply 'popping' the fly across the surface an inch or so at a time. This method often produces a number of follows and sub-surface boils, but continue to retrieve in exactly the same way, for the fish tend to lose interest if you speed up or slow down. Why, I do not know, but it happens.

A fishing pal used to say that when a fish was following your fly you should keep on retrieving, look away, and wait for it to take. But only someone like him would be able to ignore the sight of a trout homing on to a fly which would be its downfall only if the angler got it right!

An early-season rainbow trout taken from a small stillwater, Lynch Hill, Oxfordshire, England. This is a beautiful fish, but it is marked by its badly damaged tail. This water always responded well to both dry-fly and wake-fly techniques. Sadly, it has now closed as a trout fishery.

FISHING WET FLIES

With the wet fly it is usual to fish a team of three or four, a couple being imitation patterns, one an attractor and the top one on the leader, known as the 'bob', a bushy model. Wet flies are effective throughout the year but they are particularly so in the warmer months. They vary in size, the most common being 10s, 12s and 14s and are generally smaller than lures. The wet fly is most effective when fished on a floating line on an overcast day where there is a ripple on the water. As with nymphs, the actual depth at which the wet fly must be fished is absolutely critical. I have known days when even the length of the leader dictated whether or not fish would be caught.

Undoubtedly, the most popular wet fly currently in use is the Soldier Palmer when fished as the bob. It is not my favourite, but some anglers always have one on their cast. Other patterns which are highly successful are the Dunkeld, Invicta, Silver Invicta, Butcher, Greenwell's Glory and all the other traditional patterns: it is a return to the long-established flies. The flies should be set on the cast with about a yard (1m) between each dropper, with the droppers not too long, 4–6in (10–15cm) is my preference.

There will be days when things go wrong and the leader will tangle itself again and again and when that first serious knotted mess occurs and a kink has appeared in the line the best advice is to change the entire leader. It takes time but it will restore efficient fishing and remove the frustration and aggravation which happens when your leader insists on tangling itself. Repeatedly untangling it takes time and drains one's patience, so change it. Most flyfishermen carry spare leaders already made up, but I prefer to use line straight from the spool as and when I need a fresh leader.

It is of paramount importance that the patterns of the individual wet flies have relevance to their position on the cast. The bob-fly is usually palmered, such as a Soldier Palmer or Grenadier; on a three-fly cast, the next one down would be an attractor such as a Dunkeld or Bloody Butcher, and on a cast with four flies an imitation such as the Greenwell's Glory or Ginger Quill, the attractor being the third fly. The point fly is again an imitative pattern, a Bibio or a sedge type. It is not essential to include light and dark patterns on the same cast and indeed it can be a distinct disadvantage.

What the angler is trying to do is bring the trout to the cast with an attractor so that it either takes that fly or one of the imitative patterns. The bob-fly is positioned to fish right up in the surface and to catch the eye of the trout there and if it can be held steady it can prove to be highly successful.

Trout usually respond to a slow, steady retrieve, but as at all other times when the fish are uncooperative it might be necessary to try whizzing the flies back towards you. This has been known to produce that long-awaited savage pull and as you lift the line from the water you connect with the solid resistance of a sizeable trout in its native environment.

Although four flies to a cast is not always allowed and is not that popular, there is much to be said for it.

The extra fly behind the bob-fly means that the team of flies provides more resistance in the water, therefore the bob-fly can be fished 'on the dibble' for a longer period without the weight of the fly line or the wind affecting it quite as much as it would if there were fewer flies on the cast. I have found that the more flies there are on the cast, the smaller their size should be. They are more effective smaller, and also casting will be easier, with fewer tangles.

There are many occasions when it is not possible to deduce accurately from the activity of the trout which food (or even type of food) they are feeding on. On this type of day it is a great advantage to be fishing a wet fly. It is easier to match the natural due to the many patterns, and the smaller sizes in which they (usually) come. Additionally, a splash of colour or flashy material

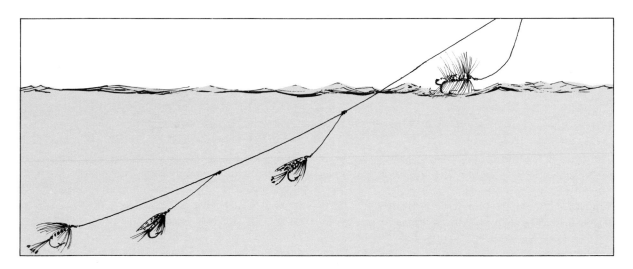

Four flies allow the bob-fly to be 'dibbled' more efficiently.

might attract them into taking. If a large fly were used, the chances are that the fish which are feeding up in the water would refuse it, and possibly move away altogether.

The crucial factor affecting the catch rate is the depth at which the trout are feeding. If there is much activity at the surface, the chances are very fair that a floating line, with the flies fishing high in the water, will be effective, but this is not always the case. Sometimes a fish will rise to the surface only once. The better fish to go after are those that can be seen rising regularly, as they can be intercepted. If they take the fly, it is simply a matter of spooning their stomach contents to see what they are feeding on.

One day that I spent with a friend on a large reservoir illustrates this very well. We set off from the jetty, and had not motored far when we realized that fish were rising all around us. We cautiously skirted the area on low power and set the boat to drift down a slight wind lane. We saw many fish rising, but those that actually took the fly were not the ones we had cast to, with all but a very few exceptions. I was first into a fish on a Green Pea, and several more followed. Graham was not meeting with such success until I handed him a Green Pea, which produced a fish on his first cast. Upon checking the stomach contents of our fish, we found that they were feeding heavily upon Daphnia rather than on adult Buzzers.

After lunch we returned to the water to find that the weather had brightened and the fish were no longer rising. The Daphnia had obviously gone down in the water, but because of our success in the morning we decided to try some fresh scenery and headed for the far side of the water. Here, in a large bay, fish rose everywhere with increasing frequency, and proved to be virtually uncatchable. Because the sun was out, we scaled down the strength of the leaders and reduced the fly sizes, and produced one fish to a Silver Invicta.

When fish are feeding at the surface, it is often a matter of trial and error to ascertain the 'winning team' of wet flies, but when they are deeper it often becomes harder. When fishing at the surface, the most important factors to consider are the clarity of the water, and the brightness of the day. The clearer the water and the brighter the day, the smaller the fly should be. The leader should be matched accordingly. I do not agree that a bright fly should be used on a bright day. I think that when this adage was first coined, a 'bright' colour would have been our idea of a dull orange or similar. I am certain that modern fluorescent colours should not form a major part of a fly dressing on a bright day. On such a day, subtlety is needed.

When using a sinking line, however, bright colours can be used. When fish are feeding on Daphnia, a fly with a certain amount of fluorescence will enhance its effectiveness. If the water is clear, fly sizes should still be kept small. It is only necessary for the trout to see the fly, and it can do so more easily in clear water and in bright conditions, so it is not necessary to present the fish with a full and glorious technicolour version.

FISHING A LURE

This is perhaps the most emotive subject in fly-fishing because it is derided by many anglers as lacking in thought and application, but in some respects it demands more application than any other technique. There is no doubt that at some stage in his career every flyfisherman has used a lure as a last resort when the trout have ignored all the flies which have been offered, even though the angler has given the matter much thought. With other anglers the lure is the only way of fishing they know, but between these extremes there lies a compromise which should be understood and accepted by all stillwater flyfishermen.

It must be said at this juncture that not all waters allow the use of a lure and even when they may be used their size might be restricted. The rules must be found out before fishing, and this is of course always the first and obligatory consideration.

The term 'lure' has come to apply to any fly which is not representative of the insect species upon which trout feed as part of their natural diet. If this is taken literally it can be accepted, but some lures represent the fish fry which trout also feed on, others mimic leeches.

The truth is that on stillwaters many more large trout are taken on lures than on small flies, but nymphs, wet and dry flies also account for many large trout and so the key word must be versatility. If the angler is able to recognize that more than one method is worthy of consideration on the day then his chances will be improved. He can so easily furiously cast flies at rising trout and have them repeatedly ignored. On some occasions it is possible to match the hatch, but many evenings spent casting to uninterested trout can only end in total frustration. I am convinced that whatever the conditions and however the trout that can be seen are behaving, there are many fish out of sight which are feeding on the bed of the lake or reservoir. Fishing for these trout will provide results which could not be bettered on the day.

Then, having decided to fish for these trout of the sub-surface inclination there are further choices on offer and many considerations. The time of year is just as important as it is when fishing with the floating line and with nymphs or wet flies. In early season, with cool water, the fly should be small and I always like one with a lot of black in its dressing and with an even smaller dropper, possibly totally different in colour. White is an obvious and popular choice but on many occasions an orange fly can trigger off the necessary aggression in a trout.

Perhaps at this time it might be appropriate to discuss the constitutions of a lure and some of the logic behind its use.

The trout is faster than most other fish species and therefore requires more food. On those days when the trout seem to be completely off their feed the reason is that the water temperature has risen to a point where the fish is unable to take in enough oxygen to maintain its search for food. These days are always calm because wind action on the water increases its oxygen content. Trout inactivity can also be induced by the presence of an unwanted chemical agent in the water but this has a far more dramatic effect than do ordinary weather conditions.

However, under normal circumstances trout can be tempted to take a fly for reasons of food, curiosity or aggression. They will never take a fly through fear and alarm, so these two instincts have to be avoided, though how an angler does this constantly is beyond the author.

A brace of Australian rainbows. Many dream of trout fishing in the prolific waters and idyllic surroundings provided by Australia. For some, this dream came true when the World Fly Fishing Championships were held there in 1988.

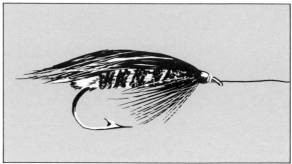

A mobile-winged fly. It opens out (left) when the pause comes in the retrieve, and slims down when pulled

(right). This creates a pulsating effect as the fly moves through the water.

Many trout take a lure imitating a small fish because they naturally feed on fish fry. The trout will also take a lure fished deep and slow, which they mistake for a bottom-crawling leech, another of their natural food items. Trout do not take a brilliantly coloured orange Whisky Fly because they see it whizzing around the water regularly, they take it because it arouses their aggression and curiosity. Once a trout has been hooked and lost on a garish fly, the best chance of taking that fish will be on an imitative pattern, and I believe that it will never again be tempted to take a lure similar to that on which it was hooked and broke away if that lure is retrieved in the same way as previously.

The trout's attention is not only attracted by bright colours, the fish can be 'turned on' by glittering materials and those that have movement, such as marabou substitute. A perfect example of this is the unique diving and darting action of a fly weighted at the head. Size of lure can also be an attraction to trout but this is more prevalent during the latter end of the season when the waters have been warmed.

It is usual to fish a lure on a sinking line but this is not always the case. Sometimes, when the water is shallow, a floating line or a sinking-tip line will be more effective when above the trout, for example when the Muddler Minnow is worked on a floating line to create a wake, – a technique which is deadly on some occasions but unproductive on others.

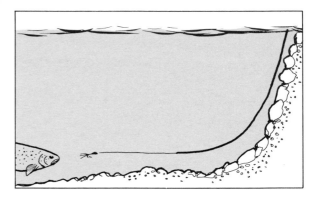

A trout which cruises after the fly is often spurred into action as the fly starts to come up the bank at the end of the retrieve.

Fishing with a sinking line

Lines are available in a wide range which sink at varying speeds, but I do not like a fast-sinking line unless I am fishing from a boat or I want the fly to fish hard on the bottom, where I know that there is no weed and it is free from obstruction – but there are not many waters like this. When my lure is fishing the bottom of the water I want it to be just far enough above the weed and obstructions so that I can fish out the whole cast without snagging, which would frighten away any trout in the area that might be interested in taking the fly.

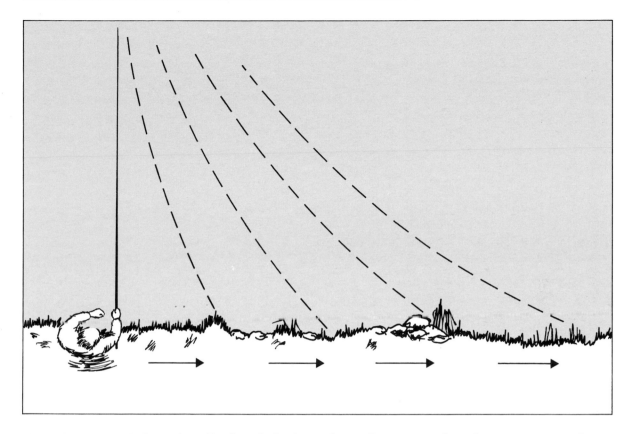

The angler retrieves the line as he walks along the bank.

My three favourite lines are one of neutral density, a medium-sinking line and one with a copper core. My contention is that if a line is sinking while it is being retrieved the presentation of the fly is wrong. I try to fish at a level depth with a sinking line, in other words I allow the line to sink to the correct depth and then retrieve it at that depth right through the cast and until the fly is forced to rise at the end. Its rising through the water is a crucial point in flyfishing, for if a trout is following the fly, or even if it has just seen it, the fish is more likely to take the fly immediately it starts its ascent or even as it is about to be lifted from the surface. The trout's reason for these actions is aggression, although curiosity and hunger may combine and compel it to take the fly.

Deciding which line and fly to use is as much of a problem when lure fishing as it is with any other style. Sadly, lure fishing has become known as a chuck-it-and-chance-it method because anglers use so many different styles and means of working them. Lures are often just cast out as far as possible and retrieved in any fashion and this fails more times than any other method, for the only time a trout might be hooked is when it makes an impulsive grab as the fly speeds past. But there are ways to make lure fishing subtle and here forethought and application are important.

The effectiveness of allowing the wind to take a floating line round has already been described (page 24). As the wind moves the line into a bow the retrieve is neither straight into the bank nor across the wind, an action which can make a trout investigate the fly. With a sinking line, of course, one cannot use the wind in this way, other than with a very slow-sinking line under conditions of strong wind, but it is possible to simulate this retrieve if you have enough bank room. It is possible to curl a retrieve with a fast- or slow-sinking line, but it is easier with a slow- or medium-sinker. The effect is to bring the fly to the bank where there is no angler's silhouette looming into the vision of any trout following the fly right the way back. The fly will also change direction by 'turning a corner' and receive a burst of speed, both of which compel a hungry trout

into lunging at your offering. This method cannot be employed if bank space is restricted, or there are obstructions, but it still works as well for me today as when it was first demonstrated by a well-known flyfisherman in my early trout-fishing days.

It is a simple technique whereby the cast is made at right angles and the line allowed to sink to the required depth. As the retrieve commences, the angler walks backwards, slowly, whilst pointing the rod down the line. The fly eventually fishes out away from the angler and commits itself to many angles during the retrieve. Takes may come anywhere during the retrieve, even right in at the bank.

There are times when you are forced to take station somewhere on the bank and fish there, but

Above *An angler fishing with a lure on a northern England reservoir. Note the disturbance that the line has created on the calm surface. This type of surface makes floating-line fishing difficult in the absence of a rise.*
Right *A stillwater rainbow trout is brought safe into the waiting net.*

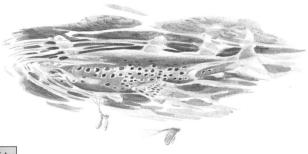

it is not the end of the world and with some forethought your day's fishing can be as rewarding as it would have been if you had had your choice of bankspace. Simple observation is always a necessity, for instance you should know that in cool conditions the trout are likely to be lying deeper and at the 'tail' of the wind, and if it is warm the fish might be anywhere, very possibly within a few feet of the surface or lying on the bottom.

In my view, fish do not seek food in mid-water unless there is a large supply of daphnia present, or if freak weather conditions (such as aeration) have forced them there. These points do not apply when the water is shallow, when a sinking line is not necessary, and my opinion is that the ideal depth for fishing with a sinking line is about 8ft (2.5m). At this depth the whole area can be covered so that any trout in the vicinity will see the fly. If the water is much deeper I fish either at the surface or on the bottom.

The retrieve with a sinking line is all-important because the lure may work better at a particular speed. In general terms, a bright or flashy fly should be fished faster than a drab one.

Confidence tells me to fish a lure with a slow retrieve, which also allows me to feel for the takes which might come from one of those cautious trout which usually ignore a fast-moving fly. Very often a trout will pluck at the fly two or three times before it eventually takes, so that it is vital that one does not make the strike until the fish is felt pulling against the retrieve. A useful tip is to watch the small belly of line falling from the rod-tip to where it enters the water. The slack there remains between pulls of the retrieve but if a trout takes the fly as the line is released prior to being retrieved again, the line, instead of falling slack, will stay taut to the water, thereby notifying the angler of events at the end of the line.

The reason why the trout will take as the fly stops is very probably because the movement pattern has changed, the fly momentarily sinking, starts to rise and move forward as the retrieve resumes. If the trout has already taken, this could also mean the setting of the hook. I feel sure, also, that the darting and lifting movements of the normally retrieved fly are associated by the trout with previous encounters when they have broken free. Neither is it only the colour of the fly that can alarm them, but also the artificial's shape and style of retrieve.

Some flyfishermen use the figure-of-eight retrieve, others will tuck the rod under their arm and draw the line back with a motion similar to that of milking a cow, but while both the traditional and the 'underarm' methods provide a consistent retreive I am convinced that the angler is not fully in control if the rod is not held properly in order that it is raised at the correct instant.

During the retrieve the angler must always have that sense of being in control as the fly returns. This can be done by pointing the rod-tip down the line, so that if a fish takes it can be detected immediately. Use the index finger of the rod-holding hand to trap the line and feel for pulls. It can be held down quickly to apply sufficient pressure on the trout to set the hook. The rod must then be lifted immediately to allow you and the rod to play the fish, the rod and line acting as the buffer and allowing you to apply pressure as needed.

There may be anomalies with regard to striking, an important subject which often calls for thought. We all know that the strike must be made when the trout has the fly firmly in the jaw, but I did not know how important this was until a few years back. I had broken my ankle and since I was not totally disabled I continued fishing. But then I realized that I was missing many chances and could not understand why. I sat down and thought about this because I knew that I could do better.

Then the answer came to me. I was favouring one foot when standing on the slope of a reservoir bankside, so that when a trout took I was striking across my body instead of lifting the rod vertically. The next time a take occurred I corrected my position and hooked the trout. From then on I only missed takes when I forgot to stand properly.

When I am fishing with lures I prefer a shooting head because it gives me confidence. On the retrieve the line is straighter to the rod-tip because all the weight is forward, and I also feel the takes better through the backing, which makes it easier to quickly tighten on the fish. There will be similar arguments to substantiate the use of weight-forward line, but this kind of line offers more resistance and becomes a nuisance when the shooting part of the line begins to crack up, which seriously impairs its casting ability. The most important problem is in selecting a compatible backing line that enables the angler to keep his

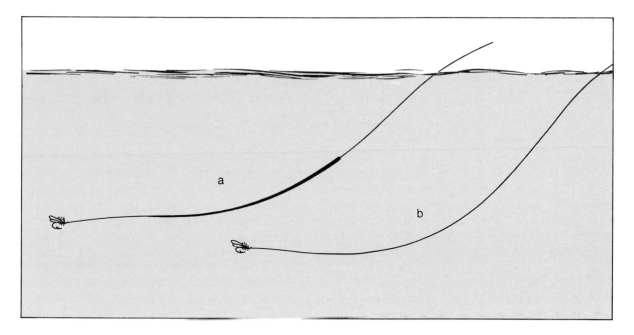

temper and some are not conducive to this!

After experiments with many types of backing I still prefer the flat monofilament. It must be well stretched before use and I prefer a moderate colour, not those pinks and oranges that are available. They may work well for some anglers but I am happier if every part of my tackle – and myself – is unobtrusive so far as the trout are concerned. All I want them to see is the fly and – later – my landing net.

SEASONAL CHANGES

At the start of the season I fish a small black lure for preference, unless recent experience has suggested that another selection should be made. A black and silver lure has always been effective and I fish this in early season, preferably into the wind, and deep.

As the water warms, the choice of colour becomes more important, with the brighter colours performing better and are more attractive when retrieved quickly. I do not subscribe to that old adage of a 'bright fly for a bright day'. For me, more appropriate would be a small fly on a bright day and then as evening approaches I change to a white one such as a Missionary or an Appetizer and never any of the black flies. Experience has shown this and I catch more trout by using these methods. Some of the old sayings are worth consideration, but not all of them.

I have found, too, that results are improved if the size of the fly is stepped up in the twilight hours and even when it gets darker. There is an additional point to be made here, and it is that one must be able to offer the trout a fly to which it has not been accustomed. My reasoning for this is that by the middle of every season every trout not so far caught will have seen all the standard patterns and may be conditioned to their appearance. So a fly that is undeniably different can be very useful and at the same time it forces me to muster imagination and creativity when working at the fly-tying bench.

BANKSIDE TECHNIQUE

Although it has already been stated, I repeat that all flyfishermen must surely understand and accept the most important and elementary requirement in flyfishing: that the trout should see the fly, not the fisherman. But having watched flyfishermen for many years I regret that this is not always the case. Heavy footfalls, for instance, and splashy wading are two things which announce the human presence to the trout.

Whatever kind of bankside is before you, it always pays to approach it as stealthily as possible. Having done that, the thinking angler spends a moment or two studying the water where he will be casting. If his approach has been haphazard and clumsy the fish will have been alerted and the area will be devoid of fish before he reaches the bank. The trout will eventually return, but will be more wary too.

This is most important if wading is not necessary. All movements should be deliberate and the concentration focused on spotting tell-tale signs in the water that trout are in the vicinity.

If the area chosen has to be waded in order to give more casting distance, a less-than-quiet footfall might just be acceptable, but the matter should always be one for consideration.

For many years, arguments about tackle design have occupied a lot of space in angling publications. For instance, there have been many articles about highly varnished rods being visible from afar and presumably putting trout down. But I have never seen a trout flee at the sparkle from a polished rod and this rather nebulous oldie remains open in my mind. However, all my rods have a matt finish – just in case!

Fly lines are another emotive subject. It was argued by many expert flyfishermen that a white line, being visible to the angler at a good distance, must also be just as visible to the trout. I broadly disagree with this concept but feel that it might be so on some occasions, not all. Judging by the number of brightly coloured floating lines available I must assume that many manufacturers and anglers agree with me. If a line is outlined against the light and visible to a trout, one of a light colour would be an advantage on a still day. However, on a day when the water surface is broken a darker line will be better disguised.

Many flyfishermen are using mahogany-coloured floating lines these days, but I think that this is more of an attempt to disguise their style of fishing than an example of their deductive powers. Their logic, it seems, is that if another angler sees them taking trout with a dark-coloured line it will be assumed that it is also a sinking line. This might be the case, but the line has not been chosen for the right reason.

For many years I have used white, black, pink, yellow and fluorescent green floating lines and the only time I have been aware of any differences was with the black one. I was fishing a small river and the flashing of my light-coloured line was frightening all the trout away. I changed to a black line and caught fish. On the other hand if I had changed to any other colour apart from black the result might have been the same, but I do not believe in this kind of experimentation.

Where fishing larger waters is concerned I feel that the colour of the line becomes less important unless the fish have ample time to see it. On still, bright days everything possible should be done by the flyfisherman to ensure that as much subtlety as possible is achieved. Again, one should try to see things through the trout's eyes. Any line which disturbs the water and breaks the surface film is going to be immediately apparent to the fish. The more we try to avoid this the better will be our chances of catching them.

I am never happy when fishing quiet stillwater with a floating line which produces a high profile that I can see. If it stands up on the surface it must cause more of a disturbance in the surface film in the form of a shadow, whereas a line which floats in this film becomes part of the fish's environment. If there is a substantial ripple the matter of profile is not so important.

Top *Peter Stone with the largest rainbow ever caught on the fly in the UK: 21 lb (9·5 kg), from Avington.*
Above *A popular bank spot! Anglers fishing into the wind alongside weeds at Hanningfield, Essex, England.*

BOAT FISHING ON STILLWATERS

A boat provides both versatility and solitude. With a partner in the boat, there is also an element of not-too-serious competition. In a boat, too, it is easier to 'steal up' on the trout, with very few exceptions, allowing you to fish among them wherever they are.

Whatever the reasons for taking to the water, the essential ingredient is organization. The space within a boat is very limited and so one must make plans in order to cope with the situation. Being organized also leads to a greater degree of care, for as the water over which the craft will move is usually of a substantial depth it is prudent to have regard to safety. Organization also helps towards the possibility of expensive and well-loved tackle being lost or broken.

The first consideration should be stealth, because havoc can result from the enlarged silhouette that a boat causes, and the vibrations from movements of and from within it can combine to alarm the trout.

There are some essential items needed when boat fishing:

Anchor

This is at the top of the list. You do not have to use it when an anchor is provided, but the day can be a miserable catastrophe if the conditions make it a necessity and you don't have one. Equally as bad is an inefficient anchor, for a well-designed model should have at least three flukes with a heavy shank and about 6ft (1.8m) of chain and then a weight before it is joined to a length of rope. The weight and chain keep the anchor lying as level as possible so that it grips the bottom with the long rope also helping. Do not use a thin man-made fibre rope, it might be strong enough but pulling on it with bare hands can be very painful.

Drogue

This is another item which must be properly designed. Every drogue has the same basic shape, but the larger it is the more efficient it will be. In heavy weather, when the boat pulls strongly at the drogue, a length of chain attached to the strings will help it stay deep and working properly. A rope that is longer than usual will also have

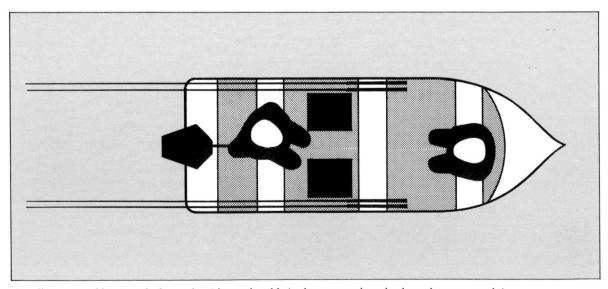

A well-organized boat: rods down the sides and tackle in the centre where both anglers can reach it.

the same effect and the two features combined will ensure that you have a very efficient model.

G-Clamps

At least one of these on board will ensure that you can anchor the boat in any position with regard to the wind and that you can position the drogue anywhere too.

These items are essential, although seats of course are necessary for disabled anglers. Some anglers consider a thwartboard an essential item, but I do not. This is an elaborate plank which fits across the gunwales and enables the anglers to fish from a higher position than the seats, at the same time helping to avoid leg-cramp and stiffness. My objection to the thwartboard is that it provides a higher-than-necessary profile, something that should be avoided.

There are also the rudimentary essentials such as clothing in anticipation of a change in the weather, and food and drink, but no experienced angler will need advice on that subject.

Having organized oneself and the boat, the next step is deciding where to commence fishing. This is the point at which familiarity with the water is of great help, otherwise one must glean as much information as possible from local anglers or officials at the fishing lodge before setting out. The fishery officers are constantly on the alert for notable catches and speak to the anglers who do well, so these officials should be in a position to offer advice on the good areas.

It is foolish not to ask for such advice because there are unseen features on all waters which make them holding areas and therefore attractive to the trout. These places are usually indicated on a map which includes the contours of the bed. Look for a place where there is a steep drop-off or where the bottom rises sharply from deep or relatively deep water and then drops off again. Another usually excellent underwater feature is a trench or the bed of an old river, which gives the same effect as a reservoir which has flooded some land.

The areas I have described above are more attractive to brown trout than to rainbows because the brown trout is more active during the darker hours, but I am certain that during the day they will feed for short bursts, so catching a large brown trout is a case of being in the right place at the right time.

Rainbows will also be attracted here because insects and water life will accumulate on raised areas and at certain times of the year there will be an inordinate number of fish there, which can be caught before they change their feeding pattern.

To us this will seem like a change in the trout's feeding pattern, but it is due to fishing pressure. It is a point to consider where certain areas have been fished hard. If an area of the lake or reservoir is known by everyone to have fished well, that area will come under concentrated pressure and the smaller the area the greater will be the effects of hard fishing, causing an 'imploding' effect.

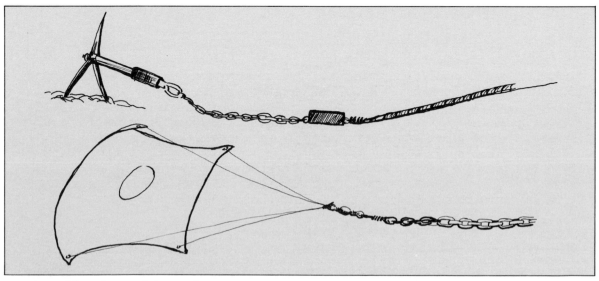

Top *A suitable anchor, and* above *a drogue.*

In a water that has few features, the fish tend to hug any that there are. In the absence of local knowledge, drifting is the most effective way of finding where the fish are lying.

Now, as soon as anglers begin fishing the trout will become more shy and then go off feed. It gives the impression that they have moved away, but it is not always the case, and good boatmanship, guile and stealth, can put anglers into position over them. One careless movement or a lost fish can change the situation immediately, but there is always satisfaction in taking a fish that has proved difficult and demanded stalking before it is at last hooked and captured.

The actual place where to fish may not be very obvious and local knowledge might be unobtainable, so various techniques will have to be tried to find fish.

BOAT FISHING TIPS

It should be taken into account that using a boat will place the occupants in potential danger, and the degree of danger is related to the organization in, and handling of, the boat. For this reason, safety should be considered before even stepping into the boat. Most waters sensibly insist on buoyancy aids being worn by boat-users. I am sure that their colour is not a disadvantage to the angler if a low profile is maintained. In any event, standing in the boat whilst fishing is undesirable: not only is it unsafe, it also presents a high profile to the fish, not to mention the exaggerated casting movement it induces.

□ On reaching the jetty ensure that the boat is fully equipped.

□ Step into the boat carefully, without over-reaching, and keep in a central position.

□ Have your boat partner pass in the equipment and tackle. Lay the bulky, non-essential items in the centre, and lay the rods along the gunwhales.

□ Ensure that movement along the boat can be achieved without stumbling over any equipment.

□ Lay the landing net(s) in a position where they, or it, can be easily reached by both parties.

□ Decide on the destination and start the engine, after first ensuring that it is in neutral gear. It is then safe to untie the anchorage and make off.

ANCHORING TIPS

□ Always approach the intended anchoring spot from upwind, and without the use of the engine, if possible.

□ Have the anchor ready to drop and ensure that the rope will uncoil without problems.

□ Drop the anchor quietly if possible.

□ Do not anchor broadside onto the wind on a leeward shore.

□ Anchor in such a way, if possible, that both occupants' flies are in the air *outside* the perimeter of the boat.

□ Anchoring the boat at a point between the bow and the middle will reduce the tendency to swing.

□ If anchored near a leeward bank, ensure that the engine is in neutral and running before the anchor is lifted.

Setting off for the day on Rutland Water. The conditions on the water are superb; but the sky is a little bright, which could send the fish deeper in the water, making them more difficult to locate.

DRIFTING AND SIDECASTING

This is the most effective way of covering an area of water. The great advantage of fishing from a drifting boat is that fresh water is always being covered and with the sidecasting technique too a very large area is available. It is just a matter of finding the depth at which the trout will take.

In modest wind conditions this method will be more comfortable than it would be if the wind were strong. For reasons of personal comfort and safety the boat is better if it is set to drift with the point downwind. If it is allowed by the fishery, I prefer to be able to attach a rudder to the stern of the boat. This enables the craft to be guided along any bank or bottom contour which might be holding trout. If a rudder is allowed and the boat is engine-driven, the engine should be lifted from the water because it can affect the action of the rudder.

If rudders are not allowed, a drogue fixed to the stern will hold the boat on a course with the bows downwind, but the steering effect will not be present and therefore wind direction is crucial. If the wind is particularly strong the boat may well drift too quickly on a rudder and the only way to fish at an effective speed would be to put the drogue out from the stern.

There are certain permutations of tackle and fishing conditions which can counter almost any weather but as a start we shall assume that the wind is moderate and that there is a pleasant day's trout fishing ahead.

First, it must be understood that a boat drifting with the bows downwind will drift faster than a boat broadside on, and that a craft with a rudder will also drift faster than one with a drogue. So remembering the direction of the wind we must consider where to commence fishing. I would select a bank with the wind blowing along it so that the longest possible drift can be achieved. There is no point in going for a sidecasting drift near the leeward shore when the drift will be finished quickly. The point of drifting and sidecasting is to locate fish and if you know that they are near the leeward shore a different method must be employed.

A rudder enables the boat to be steered into all the bank contours but without one a drogue will have to do. Some boats have engines which will steer the craft well enough and those with inboards always have rudders.

It is usual to use a sinking line when sidecasting, although a floating one will be deadly when the fish are taking on the surface. The point to remember is that the rate of drift will probably mean that the fly will be fishing quite fast, and with a floating line and a buoyant or unweighted fly the lures can skate across the top. This is not effective because most of the time a trout will ignore a fly skittering over the surface film or creating a wake *across* the wind.

If the fish are feeding very near to the surface or on it I use another method and if it is not sidecasting I employ a line with a very slow sinking speed or one of neutral density. When the fish cannot be seen and if I know that I am over water about 10ft (3m) deep or deeper I use a fast-sinking line. Remember, boat fishing makes the choice of line imperative but when the boat is drifting at a moderate speed a fast-sinking line can be controlled effectively either by stripping the line immediately the cast has hit the surface, or paying out line to allow it to sink as the boat drifts past. The rate of retrieve can also be controlled. When the boat is drifting away from the line it can be either held or retrieved as the angler wishes.

This method is made effective because, ideally, each angler casts at right angles to the boat and across the wind. If each angler is capable of casting 30 yards (27.5m) in the conditions it means that a swathe of 60 yards (55m) of water can be covered. This will find fish provided that the flies are the right pattern and are fishing at the correct depth. It is the point where two heads are better than one, for each angler can use a line with a different sinking speed. One, for instance,

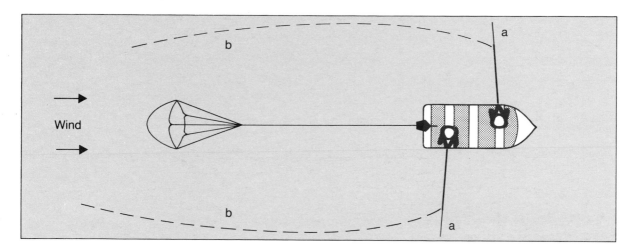

A drogue positioned at the stern controls the rate of drift and provides stability. A line cast at right angles to the boat (a) is eventually retrieved from position (b).

might use a medium-sinker and the other a fast-sinking line. The outcome will be that if the angler with the slower-sinking line fishes at the right depth both anglers will know where the fish are. If the flies were not at the correct depth the fish will not be found if they were lying deeper. But the angler with the fast-sinking line can allow his line to sink to the bottom and then retrieve it, knowing that if the trout are anywhere between the bottom and the surface his fly will pass by them.

I prefer to fish for trout with a fly that I can retrieve levelly through the water and very often the fast-sinking line will find the trout, then a line with a slower sinking rate can be used to keep the fly at the proven depth. If the boat is drifting quickly it is always necessary to use a faster-sinking line than one would use from an anchored or slowly drifting boat; in angling terms the tackle is being stepped up.

The main effect of sidecasting is to bring the fly round in the same way as 'walking up the bank'. The fly rises in the water and comes round the 'bend' and at the same time puts on a burst of speed, which should be irresistible to the trout because it resembles their natural food taking evasive action.

Unless both anglers are agreed on obvious choices, different lines and flies should be tried. The possibilities do not differ from bank to boat but the options may because deeper water can be covered from boats and therefore larger flies have more effect.

In the cool days of early season, small, dark lures are an obvious choice, then as the season progresses larger patterns become more effective.

Daphnia (of which there are three species), are better known as water-fleas and are sometimes seen in clouds in the water. They form part of the plankton population and are carried about in the water by its movement. This tiny crustacean reacts to light, rising towards the surface when it is dark and sinking back as the light fades. Being carried about by water movement, daphnia are usually found under a leeward bank, blown there by the wind. However, if calm conditions have prevailed and the weather is bright, daphnia can spread throughout the water. The chances of encountering daphnia are greater if the angler is fishing from a boat.

Trout feed greedily on daphnia but they seem never to undergo the total preoccupation with this tiny crustacean that they do with hatches of mayfly, or caenis, for instance. At other times the trout can readily be taken and the best flies to use are orange or white lures. The difficult part, as always, is to locate the area and the depth at which the trout are feeding.

This is the point at which a drifting boat has an enormous advantage, because it can be taken over fish. The next important element is depth, followed by fly pattern and size.

If an area is found to be holding trout, the drift inevitably will be fished out since the boat is moving and the fish are not. The drift will also end when the bank is reached, and so for one of the above reasons the drift has to be restarted. There are two ways of doing this, in nonchalant

style straight back along the course you came, or stealthily by moving round outside the area and recommencing the drift. This is the slower method, but it is also more sensible.

Perhaps it is unnecessary to say so, but one should never open the engine throttle fully in order to move back up-wind if fish have been located. With engines in mind, I have found that inboard engines seem to frighten away trout more than outboards. Perhaps it is because an inboard makes the whole boat tremble and thump, sending more vibrations through the water. Inboards, however, do not appear to be as popular on trout lakes and reservoirs as they used to be, and if fish can be left in their area undisturbed, with nothing to do but feed, they are more likely to be caught.

Of course, disturbance by man or boat is far more troublesome in shallow water than in deeper areas. If a water holds a good head of brown trout it is worth remembering that during the lighter periods of the day these fish will lie deeper than the rainbows. If the day is dull the brown trout may be caught in shallower water. One fishery officer told me that with echo-sounding equipment he found that browns prefer to stay over deeper water near a drop-off and the larger fish are never nearer the surface than 25–30ft (7.5–10.5m).

Here is a problem, because it suggests to me that when the fish are located by flyfishermen trout will ignore all offerings during the 'dormant' periods. The reason for this is probably due to the cannibalistic nature of the trout and their instinctive disregard for anything not sizeable enough to replace the energy expended in chasing and catching it. But as usual there are exceptions to the rule and many large brown trout have been taken on small flies. These were almost certainly in exactly the right place at the right time so that the fish did not need to deviate from their course to sip them in. It is another reason for using large lurcs when fishing deep water from a boat, particularly if there are brown trout in the area.

Page 66 *An angler quietly drifts amongst typical southern English scenery on a small stillwater.*
Page 67 Top *Drifting loch-style, with an ideal ripple on the water. This method is a very effective way of covering a large area of water.*
Page 67 Lower *Just about ready to start a loch-style competition at Grafham Water, Cambridgeshire.*

The fact that lures larger than normal flies are significantly successful from a drifting boat means that the tackle will differ from that normally used on an average bank-fishing session.

When boat fishing I usually take two rods of about 10ft (3m), one carrying a fast-sinking line and the other a slow-sinker, even a sinking tip or floating line, because it is easier to change my fishing style and safer than clambering about in the boat while changing the line on the rod.

It is essential that the rod is powerful, because you may be fishing deep and your rod needs power to set a hook into a trout when the depth of water adds considerable drag to the line. Drifting is another reason for fishing with a powerful rod, for you are more exposed to the wind and casting with a floppy rod would be hazardous. With regard to casting, whenever possible it is better and safer to make sure that both anglers' false casts are kept outside the boat but this can be difficult for the angler at the stern when he is using a rod that does not have a stiff action.

If opposite sides of the boat are to be covered, a right-handed caster at the stern will have the wind blowing over his right shoulder. This means that the rod will need to be held farther out in order to keep the fly away from him. In this position and if the wind is strong it is inadvisable to reach for distance, for it is unnecessary and unsafe. The longer the fly is in the air the more it is affected by the wind and it might become a danger to either angler. If the conditions are right and the boat has been handled properly over open water there will be fish near the boat, so it is better to carry on under improvised conditions than have to sit out the rest of the day in a casualty ward waiting to have a hook removed from some part of the person.

If the material used in the construction of the rod does not matter, a rod with a tip action will prove ideal on blustery days or when you are fishing deep. On occasion, I still use some of my tried and trusty glass-fibre rods, usually through nostalgia more than for practical reasons, but they still catch fish. The carbon-fibre (or graphite) rods are superior if they are of the right design. It is very easy to buy an inferior carbon rod because it is cheap and while there are few bad rods, some are infinitely superior to others.

I find carbon-fibre superior because its comparatively smaller diameter helps it to cut through the wind. This can be very important at the end of

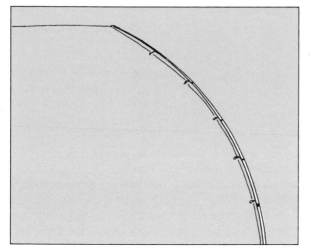

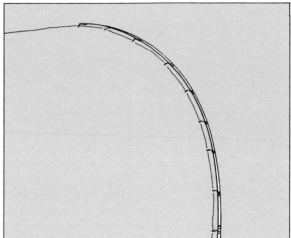

a long day during which very many casts have been made. Because the depth is crucial, a heavier line will probably be used and a carbon-fibre rod will be an asset because it 'recovers' quickly when under pressure, which means that the rod will do more of the work and relieve the angler.

The ability of carbon-fibre rods to recover quickly is also an advantage on the strike when fishing through a fair depth of water and at some distance from the boat. However, that same characteristic of carbon-fibre has to be allowed for when a fish takes the fly very close to the boat. On these occasions a hard strike with such a rod will practically always result in the fly being torn away from the trout unless it has it well inside the mouth. In other words, the force used to set the hook on the strike is proportional to the volume of water between the line and the surface, with other factors having an effect too, such as stretch in the line and the action of the rod. One might add the size of the lure, but in my opinion the force required will be largely immaterial if the hook is as sharp as possible.

In this respect, I regularly check my flies for the following points:

☐ To ensure that the fly has not twisted and is still fishing correctly.

☐ There are no knots in the cast.

☐ The hook point remains and that it is still razor-sharp. If the hook is not so, I hone it with an

Above left Tip-action rod
Above Through-action rod

Arkansas stone or fine file.

With reference to the boron rods which are now sweeping the market I have used them and find them delightful. In their action most of them remind me of the old split-cane and yet even in their serenity they have the strength of carbon-fibre. Casting is made easier with a good boron rod than with any other material I have used.

There is not much of importance with regard to lines, nor is there anything to add to what I have said in the bank-fishing section. For boat-fishing I prefer a shooting head but it can be tiresome in a boat if the backing is prone to tangling and the backing will continually catch any protuberance or obstacle in the boat. If the wind is strong it whirls round in the bottom of the boat taking line with it and frustrating many a good cast. The only way to prevent this is to have a little water in the boat, it holds the backing down and keeps it running through the rod rings much more smoothly than if it is dry.

I am aware that there is a good argument for the use of a full fly line but I am convinced that contact with the fly is much more subtle with a shooting head, allowing the strike to be made a little sooner. Once you have seen a trout eject a fly you realize that there lies the difference between a lost trout and one in the net.

DRIFT TROLLING

My inclusion of this method may attract the anger of those who disapprove of it, and my description of it will upset those who practise it. The fact is that drift-trolling is tantamount to trolling and it produces a high number of large trout. The essentials for drift-trolling are a long drift, preferably deep water and a boat with a rudder.

I have used the method on a large British reservoir with tremendous success, but it is employed only when wind conditions are too uncomfortable to fish normally in the area where I know the trout to be. The tackle required is usually heavy and the flies large, which is one of the reasons why many large brown trout fall to the style. It enables the angler to use flies which although they may be quite legitimate are not castable. A very fast-sinking line is required, the kind used in sea trolling being ideal because it has a heavy lead core and is usually coloured at 10-yard (9-m) intervals.

The boat is set at the top of the wind so that a very long drift is possible over an even depth of water. The line is paid out so that it gets down to the required depth. All the angler has to do then is hold on and wait for the trout. There is little or no finesse or elegance in drift-trolling but it does require experience and perception. The fly pattern and the depth at which the line must fish are of particular importance.

The conditions will have an effect on the angle of the line because in a strong wind the boat will travel faster, making the line adopt a less steep angle. On a day of gentle wind the line will angle down much more steeply, which means that less line must be paid out to fish at the same depth.

I only use drift-trolling on days with a strong wind because the heavy line needed gives better contact with a fly when the angle is less steep. At the same time, if the fly is moving past the trout fast the fish is more likely to snap at it, or chase and take it without having the time to inspect it. If the day is mild, I drift and retrieve in order to attain that speed of fly if I think it is crucial.

Some anglers whom I have seen drift-trolling also strip the lure back up to the boat and then let it slip back to its maximum depth. This has a two-fold effect, the first being that the lure searches all depths of the water and, secondly, it gives it the impression of seeking to escape through to the upper layers, an effect which gets a trout going every time it sees it. If the boat's rudder is so efficient that it enables a winding course to be steered there is a much greater chance of success, due to the lifelike impression created by the lure.

Once a concentration of brown trout has been discovered, mark the length of line being fished in order to maintain the consistency of depth for fishing.

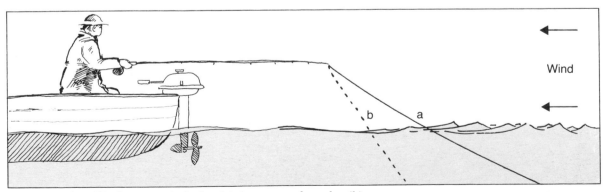

The line angle will be less on a windy day (a) than on a calmer day (b).

These anglers are looking despondent due to the calm conditions during this loch-style event.

FISHING FROM AN ANCHORED BOAT

The reasons for anchoring a boat are obvious, simply it is to hold the craft in a position to cast where the angler knows trout are feeding. The other important reason is that being anchored allows the fly to be presented to the fish in a manner which ensures they will see it and will become interested. Having decided on the area, one must approach it in the correct manner, and this depends very much on the prevailing weather.

I consider anchoring a boat either when the weather is hot and calm, or when it is very windy – two ends of the weather scale. If it is hot, bright and calm I seek a holding spot for the fish, probably in deep water, but if it is cool and windy, without hesitation I travel downwind and anchor near the leeward shore. This occurs normally in early season when the water is cooler and the fish will stay near the leeward bank because the food and warmer water are there. The water also holds more oxygen at the bottom of the wind. It is on these days that an anchor which efficiently holds the bottom is invaluable.

A classic example of this was on a reservoir in Essex. The wind was strong and then later in the day the wardens erected a red warning flag signifying that boats should stay in a safe place and not travel because of the vicious wind. We had tried an anchorage point which produced nothing and then decided to travel all the way down the wind to the dam wall. It was blowing slightly along and into the wall and the towers there formed a corner with the dam and floating rubbish was collecting there. It was definitely not a typical English spring day of the kind that inspires poetry. It was cold and very windy even though it was May.

I stopped the engine up-wind from where we would be fishing and then drifted into position, dropping the anchor so that a long rope would be necessary to get us there. When the boat had settled I tried a cast, more to stretch the backing than for any other reason – and I had an immediate take as the fly sank. We were over 50ft (15m) of water and it shelved very steeply from the bank and that take led me to assume that the trout were high in the water. Then I discovered why – the next cast was given more attention and I fished it properly. A take, a dashing fight and a beautiful silver rainbow of about 2½lb (1kg) was in the net.

There was no need to spoon this trout because its mouth was brimful with daphnia. The wind had blown it into the corner and it was high in the water because of the dull condition. Daphnia always act this way, rising because of the lack of light and being carried along by wave action. The rainbows were concentrated here and it was easy to complete a double limit of sparklingly healthy rainbow trout of a good average size, in spite of the fact that they were last season's fish and had become 'educated'.

These trout moved about in the vicinity and it was necessary to leave the area undisturbed for a while. At times a fish was contacted on a cast made at a different angle, then on returning to the original cast after a rest more trout were hooked.

On this occasion I used my own anchor because the one the Essex Water Company supplied did not have a chain or weight and I felt the anchor would not hold bottom. This was the case, because more than one boat, seeing our success, approached us and dropped anchor nearby but they were unable to contend with the wind and their anchors dragged, taking them out of the area.

On occasions like this the approach to the fishing area can be disguised by the wind and wave action, and so stealth is not quite as essential although it must never be overlooked. By taking the wind direction into account it is possible to cut the engine before reaching the fishing area and drift into it from up-wind. As you will be casting down or across the wind, the trout to be covered will not have had the boat travelling over their heads. The angler not on the engine or

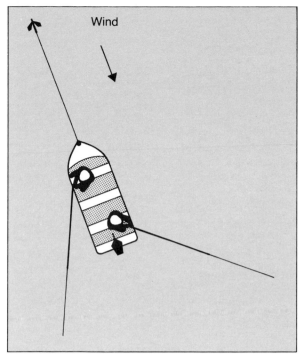

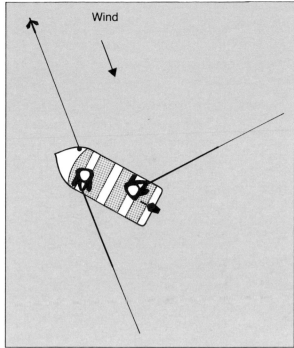

oars should have the anchor ready to drop immediately so that it reaches the bottom quickly and the boat will drift into position, taking into account the length of rope on the anchor. On a very windy day more rope is necessary so that its angle will help the anchor to bite into the bottom. I always prefer to anchor the boat from the bows because under strong wind conditions the waves are more inclined to run along the boat, whereas if it were anchored amidships the waves would push at the boat making the anchor drag.

The boat is more inclined to swing when anchored from the bows if there is a change in the wind direction. Towers of reservoirs cause the wind to swirl and I have found that by the use of a G-clamp near the bows and anchoring the boat from it the tendency to swing is reduced, although it will not stop it altogether.

On a day when the wind was blowing hard I learned a valuable lesson on a reservoir in Buckinghamshire. We had anchored the boat near the leeward bank, which is all dam wall and therefore deep. The fish seemed to be in a feeding mood and at times they could be taken in succession, then going quiet before feeding again.

Obviously there was a shoal of trout working in this area but it seemed to me that they were acting strangely. My partner and I were both on sinking

Above left A boat anchored at the point is safer in a wind but has a tendency to swing.
Above By shifting the anchor rope position slightly, stability is maintained, the tendency to swing is reduced, and it is easier and safer to cover the water.

lines and matching each other for takes and fish, when I noticed that boats to my right caught trout when we stopped taking them. Then we caught fish after a boat to our left had contacted them. It was reasonable to assume that the trout were moving from left to right but I could not believe that they were circling the complete bank of the reservoir or that the water was so full of trout that shoals were continuously passing. But the takes were very regular.

The trout we had taken were quite high in the water and so when activity stopped I began to fish deeper, knowing that the shoal had passed. I was not convinced that the fish were not responding to the weather conditions and moving out of an area where there was plenty of food. The results of my fishing deeper were that I would begin catching trout on the bottom, then it would go quiet once more. Then fish were caught higher in the water and suddenly the pattern became clear to me.

On one part of their move the fish were

travelling high in the water, then they would turn and come back deeper before turning again. This was proved by watching the boats to left and right who were catching fish consistently when the fish were higher in the water. Then when the boats to my right stopped taking trout we fished deep and soon contacted them; then the boats on the left took fish higher in the water, followed by us. The effect of it all was that we had consistent sport with those rainbows.

This experience has been repeated on other occasions and while it cannot be said to be the rule it is certainly not an exception. It was an example of the results one can obtain from watching and applying reason. There are times when we fish frantically in the belief that we are doing the correct thing and we shall soon catch a fish, but what we should do is stop and think about our actions and ask ourselves if we are using the best approach. I do this and it has a calming effect on my fishing, bringing everything back into perspective.

The fact is, trout fishing is not totally about catching fish, although on the day I have described I was certainly not there just to be soaked,

frozen and battered by the wind! In conditions like that the more active the trout the more bearable becomes the occasion.

On the kind of day described above I use two lures when boat fishing because the casting is not so arduous and the risk of tangles between fly and leader is lessened. The flies should be smaller than later in the year, probably a Size 8 longshank and the fly is always black, possibly with a silver body. When I began trout fishing, anglers relied on flashy materials such as tinsel, or yellows and orange colours, to attract the trout, but now it appears to be normal to employ fluorescent colours for attraction. These are usually incorporated in tag at the tail or throat of the fly.

Personally, I prefer the old-fashioned methods and use golds and silvers to give the fly a flashy finish. To me, it seems more natural. Of course, I do use the yellows and oranges because they

Opposite *A superb stillwater brown trout is unhooked near the dam at Rutland Water, Leicestershire. The fish was taken in deep water.*
Below *This boat is drifting, but it is in an ideal position for anchoring.*

occur naturally in the water even if they are not as brilliant as we make them. To my eyes a fluorescent fly does not look natural and might scare off any trout which is more than usually wary, and these are probably the larger ones too. I do not deny the effectiveness of fluorescent materials but I feel that if a colour or material is effective in attracting fish it can also have the opposite effect.

I have the same opinion about the 'flashabou' kind of material that is available. Although these highlight the effect of a fly in the water what is lost is the natural effect of hair or feather. I never trim the ends of a hairwing fly because it squares the ends of the fibres, but leave them naturally tapered because this streamlines the fly and leaves the natural appearance.

The artificial materials cannot be tapered in the same way as fur, which is why I leave them out of a dressing, but these are just my own prejudices and, as I have already said, confidence is all-important and an integral part of this is the fly when I am flyfishing.

I have had most success with the larger brown and rainbow trout while fishing over deep water and close to a landmark such as a draw-off or aeration tower. If I can find an area where deep water surrounds a hump rising from the bed of the water it usually forms a hot-spot. The larger trout seem to congregate in deep water, particularly in late season when these places in an otherwise apparently featureless expanse of water attract the maturing fly. They make a natural larder for the trout to feed on without expending a lot of energy.

The essentials for fishing this kind of area are, first, the stability of the boat, and here the weather must be taken into account. It is dangerous to anchor from amidships on a rough day because a broad profile is presented to the wind and waves, leading to the possibility of the boat filling with water. Secondly, unless one angler is right-handed and the other left-handed, one of the flies will be passing within the confines of the boat. I still prefer to anchor the boat from a rope attached to the thwart, a point between the bows and the first seat. It gives a small angle but still maintains a margin of safety and allows both anglers to fish to different areas.

When I am fishing over a rise in the bed of the water I prefer to anchor on the shallower part and fish into the deeper area, the flies being retrieved up the side of the hump which always seems to provide consistent results. If I am anchored near a tower I like to be able to cast past it and retrieve the fly through what should be the most productive water, of course assuming that I am on the upwind side. Ideally, I look for water about 25–30ft (7.5–9m) deep and had a firm preference for this even before the fisheries officer with the fish-location equipment told me that large fish in his reservoir always lie at about the 25ft (7.5m) contour.

Long casting, I am convinced, gives an angler a huge advantage when fishing over deep water because the fly is at maximum depth for longer and also because it is easier to keep in touch with the fly at that depth, but I do not like the sagging belly which is produced by full lines when fishing deep water. There are anglers who count to a number when they think their fly has reached the required depth. If you ask them how deep they are fishing they will say: 'I counted to fifty', or some other number. But how fast did they reach the number? The countdown method works for some, but I find it that it is boring and spoils the enjoyment of my fishing. It is easy to find the depth and sometimes I use a watch as an aid.

When fishing at greater depths I normally use a white or yellow fly, possibly because I have had more fish on those colours and have become superstitious about other colours. I prefer hairwing lures because of their flexibility and mobility in the water, which gives them more life, an effect which can also be enhanced by the use of marabou in the dressing. Tinsel or mylar is used for the body of the lure because I am trying to maximise the effect of the limited light at that depth. A bulky body of chenille might be beneficial but I would hesitate to use it if it were not enhanced by silver tinsel.

A word of warning: it is advisable to hold onto the rod while the lure is sinking because trout are likely to take on the drop. A number of fish have been caught as my fly sank and the first indication for an unwary angler would be a disappearing rod, which can be avoided by positioning the rod so that it cannot be pulled from the boat or holding on to it.

The retrieve should begin when the fly has been allowed to sink to the required depth. On occasion I have hooked a trout within the first pull of the retrieve and it has happened frequently enough to suggest that the fish was inspecting the fly as it sank and the first movement of the pull

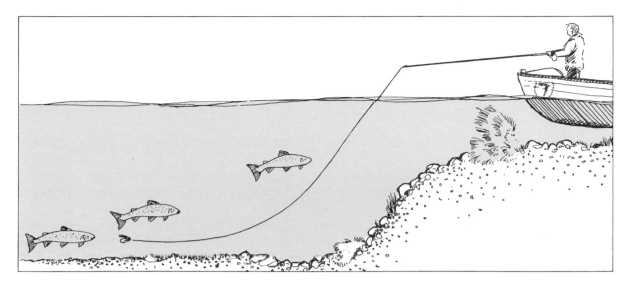

A fly retrieved up the edge of a sunken island stands a better chance of covering fish.

caused the trout to take it. Every fish I have taken this way has been a brown trout and, interestingly, all the trout that were caught on the drop have been rainbows, as far as I can recall.

I always use a slow retrieve, which means that I never use a weighted fly when fishing hard on the bottom. The intention is make the fly 'crawl' along the bottom and over obstacles, not digging itself into them. This gentle retrieve means that if the fly does hit an obstacle it will move over it instead of lodging, which could happen if the fly were being retrieved fast. The take will often come as the fly starts to move off the bottom, so the fly should be fished slowly all the way to the boat for the trout might be following it. Many a specimen brown or rainbow has come into view behind the fly with the fish's nose almost touching it, but once the boat is in sight the trout sink back into the depths. Nothing will induce the fish to take that fly, if they were going to have it they would have done so sooner.

From my observations, raising the speed of the retrieve will put the fish off, and stopping the retrieve gives the trout time to inspect the fly and put its sense of smell to work. Therefore I prefer to keep the fly moving at the same speed all through the retrieve, and there is nothing more thrilling than to see a large wild trout following a lure which you have presented to it in order to deceive and that thrill is not affected whether or not the trout takes.

There are occasions when a slow pull is felt, which could be either an obstacle or a fish and one must just continue the retrieve as before. You will soon know whether it is a fish that has taken firmly enough to be hooked and that is the time to strike. If the strike is made too early the fish will turn away fast, but if the retrieve is continued without striking and the fish has let go because it was not mouthed properly, it will take again. I have known trout to do this three or four times before they held it long enough for me to strike. There is no rule of thumb for the length of time to pass before the strike: if the trout holds on long enough for you to be able to react and strike comfortably then it should be hooked. This approach applies equally when your are dry-fly fishing.

It is always exciting to hook a fish at depth because you do not know what size it is. In most of the fisherman's tales the biggest fish have always eventually escaped, but I have caught many browns and rainbows of specimen size in deep water and they have always put up a good struggle, particularly the browns which once they have their heads down and their tails up are the most difficult fish to play for their size.

It is usually easy to establish whether or not you are fishing a worthwhile area by the activity, or lack of it. It seems hardly necessary to say so, but move off if there are no active trout where you are. If the fish are there somewhere, move just a little way or fish at a different depth. The best way to move slightly is to let out some anchor rope,

Left A large stillwater rainbow giving an angler some anxious moments!
Above These anglers have forsaken the motor, in the interests of stealth, as they search for fish in Lough Corrib, Galway, on a bright day.

because this causes the least disturbance in the water.

If you have decided to fish at a different depth, start at the deepest level first, because if you try at, say, 8ft (2.5m) off the bottom you will miss any fish on the bottom. They might see the fly without moving up to take it. If there is no contact, fish slightly higher until you find them. The fish might see the fly again at their own level and react to this by now familiar intrusion into their habitat. But if the fly is retrieved at the same level as the fish the first time it will not be in view for as long as it would be if it were overhead and the chances of a trout taking will be greater. At the same time, if the trout is a little higher off the bottom the fly coming from below on the retrieve might induce a take.

Sometimes a trout will take a fly only after it has seen it a number of times. These flies are usually imitations, not lures imitating small fish which do not bear close inspection by a trout. At these times, the fish must be treated with respect, for they have survived in the water for a number of years and have become very wary and are rarely caught by luck.

I believe that fishing from an anchored boat can provide all the versatility that a fly fisherman needs, given the right conditions, but it is essential that the water is treated with the utmost respect, and that the trout are treated with the utmost caution. I have observed on many occasions that fish moving up the wind will cease rising altogether near an anchored boat and start again after they have passed it. This renders the method inappropriate when fish are inclined to rise and move up the wind. On bright days over deep water, an anchored boat can often produce fish from the depths that could not have been reached from a drifting boat. These types of conditions must be considered as parameters for gauging the likely behaviour of the fish.

Fish which have congregated in a specific area or are moving within a defined area, can always be covered best from an anchored boat, but the boat must be far enough away from them that they are not heedful of its presence.

ETIQUETTE ON THE WATER

It is because we become engrossed in our search for trout that slight lapses of concentration occur which cause inadvertent infringements on other anglers' enjoyment of the sport. I contend that we should act with caution and consideration so that we can share the water with others. If we cannot do this we should go somewhere else.

Some anglers appear to suffer from inexperience or inconsideration and prefer to catch trout at the expense of another's comfort and enjoyment, an attitude which is unfortunate and unnecessary. A few hints and tips on boatmanship might help to correct some who err inadvertently.

The first rule in a boat is to avoid bank anglers. It is not necessary to always stay well away from the bank and I am glad that there is no rule that boats should do so on most large waters. But if bank anglers are in the vicinity, courtesy demands that they should be given consideration and left to fish consistent with the rules of the water, usually 50 yards (46m). Another point is that engines should be used sparingly or the boat rowed away so that fish close to bank anglers will not be disturbed.

Drifting itself causes few problems because the boat is not under power and will probably be on a course consistent with other craft. Most problems occur on the return up-wind in order to set the drift again. If a drift has been completed successfully it is unwise to motor straight back up the course, cut the engine and start again over the same stretch. This puts the fish down or makes them leave the area and sport is spoiled. This makes it inconsiderate to motor back up a drift which is already occupied by another boat.

Generally, a boat may come within 100 yards (91m) of another from down-wind, anything closer is an infringement unless the anglers are invited nearer. In the vicinity of fish or other anglers I suggest that low power should be the norm, and cutting across another boat's drift is unforgiveable.

Another problem is caused by drifting boats and those at anchor. I have too often seen boats drifting into a bank and catching fish, then another boat decides that this is the place to be and regardless of the proximity of other boats an anchor is dropped and the occupants start fishing at the productive points of the others' drift – and all because they want to catch trout. The result is that the first boat, legitimately drifting, is now stopped from doing so because of the obstruction of the other boat.

If the area is a particularly productive bay the problem becomes serious because the boat at anchor will have virtually taken possession, forcing the first boat to fish elsewhere. The sad part is that the boat now at anchor usually ends up catching fewer or no fish because drifting was the correct method. This kind of thing seems to be becoming commonplace and I enter a plea for anyone who condones this kind of action to consider the sport of others and to reflect on how they would react if they themselves were the victims of such behaviour.

Inevitably, an angler will be in a position where he cannot manoeuvre without coming close to another boat. Here a request for guidance and an apology should heal any possible irritation.

Always be aware of the depth of water over which you are drifting. If you become grounded in a strong wind it is practically impossible to head the boat in a direction that will take it into deeper water without causing damage or becoming stranded further. Always have the engine ready in plenty of time when you are drifting towards a bank. The problems occur on wide expanses of water when you feel safe because the boat is a long way from shore, then suddenly there is a thump and you are high and dry, right in the middle of a lake and in shallow water where a few moments before you were over several fathoms. Do not panic, but push or punt the boat until it loses contact with the bottom and then motor back the way you came until you get into deep water.

When using an engine-driven boat I always make sure that it is out of gear when I switch it off. This is a simple precaution which makes for safety and tackle saving. If you are forced to start the engine quickly the other occupant, if there is one, may still be reeling in and I have known lines to be drawn into the propeller on such occasions. The results might not be just a lost line, it can also end in a jammed propeller and a boat without power. And that can be disastrous.

By motoring in front of the drifting boat, the moving one has scattered the trout and disrupted the bay to the detriment of the sport of the fishermen in the drifting boat.

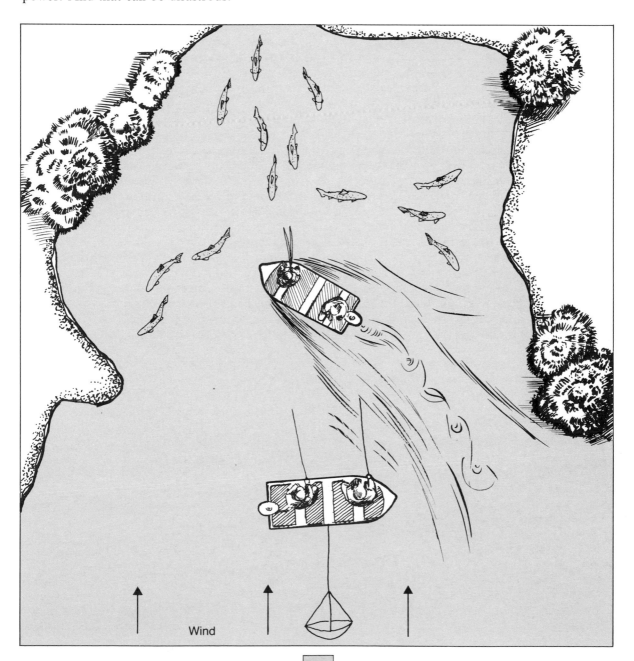

Wind

SHORTLINING LOCH-STYLE

This method has many merits and actually forms the basis for the majority of trout fishing competitions which are held on a local, national or international level. It is practised as a matter of course on the Irish loughs and Scottish lochs and in the past few years it has become the single most popular method of taking trout on most public stillwaters throughout the British Isles.

Unless the boat is particularly long, only two anglers fish, although there is sometimes a non-fishing boatman whose job, using his local knowledge, is to take the boat over water likely to yield fish. The boat is set broadside to the wind and is allowed to drift down-wind with the anglers casting directly in front of the boat. The objective is to drift onto as many fish moving up the wind as possible and in so doing the area that is being covered will always be fresh and the fish undisturbed. There was the time when only floating lines would have been used but there is a division now between those who will never use anything but a floating line and anglers who use the line that is effective on the day.

Shortlining may not seem logical to the angler who has not thought about it, but the logic is simple and irrefutable when considered objectively. If one assumes that the trout are moving upwind and the boat is moving towards them on the drift, the angler will cover fish by making a short cast. However, if you make a long cast of, say, 25–30 yards (23–27m) it is probable that you will cast over and beyond fish that have moved up towards you. As a result the trout are 'lined' and will quickly leave the area. (To 'line' a fish is to cast beyond it so that the fly line lands on or close to it and sends it away.) Once lined, a trout will not take even when covered properly. Long-casting also makes for more and longer false casts which keeps the flies out of the water, and fish are not caught when the fly is in the air.

In shortlining, the fly is lifted into the air, one false cast is made (unless the wind is strong) and then the fly is gently laid back onto the surface and fishing time is maximised. It means, too, that one can add to the enjoyment by fishing with lighter lines and rods.

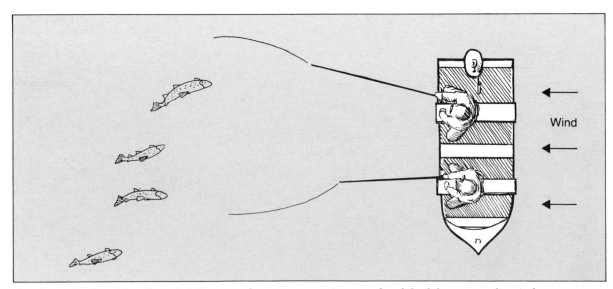

Shortlining (loch-style) will reach fish constantly, as new water is covered and the fish move up the wind.

Top *Ted Wise stocking brown trout on Coldingham Loch, Scotland.* Above *A superb brown trout taken shortlining.*

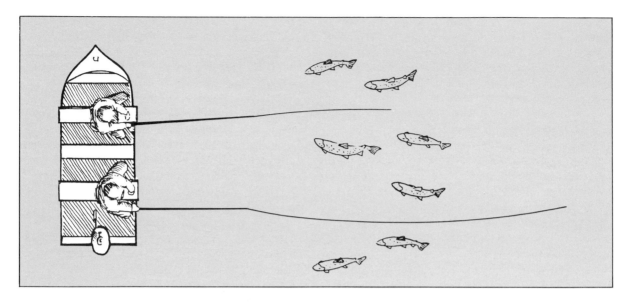

I prefer a rod of at least 10½–12ft (3–3.5m) when shortlining; a few anglers use rods substantially longer. The advantage of this is that the fly can be controlled farther away from the boat, but this is only of any consequence on a calm day or one with little breeze.

To illustrate the method described above, one of the most consistent flyfishermen I know in International flyfishing is Bob Draper, whose style differs from almost all others. He uses long casts with a heavy rod and retrieves at a fast rate before his next long cast. His success is attributable to a number of aspects of his angling, not least to his work-rate in spite of the heavy tackle.

In contrast, the style of Brian Leadbetter, World Flyfishing Champion, and possibly the world's most consistent angler, is more subtle and he daps the bob-fly most when using a floating line. But with either a floating or a sinking line his concentration is absolute. Both Draper and Leadbetter are totally exhausted at the end of a day's fishing.

Of course, there are many other very fine flyfishermen but these two represent ability of the highest class at opposite ends of the style and method range.

Fly selection when short-lining is of much more importance than some would believe. Ultimately, it is up to the individual because, I repeat, some flies which are successful will not catch fish for some anglers. For myself, I have trouble catching trout on a Soldier Palmer even though at the moment it is the most popular fly in England. I

A longer cast misses fish, whereas a short cast can be made several times with a better chance of success.

have caught very few trout on it even if it is taking fish all over the water, and in consequence I rarely have one on my cast. I have the same trouble with the Peter Ross and Alexandra, different kinds of fly, even though they catch plenty of trout for others, and the same problem exists for other highly skilled anglers.

Short-lining requires short casts, which makes it possible to use more than one fly with ease, the normal number being three, although four is a possibility if the rules of the fishery allow. For me, three flies are adequate and there is no doubt that later in the season, when the trout get to 'recognize' certain flies, they will avoid them. Sometimes two well-spaced-out flies are better than three or four and although I prefer less the usual distance between flies is about 3ft (1m) with the dropper lengths no more than 6in (15cm).

In my opinion, the point fly should be an imitation and the middle dropper, a Dunkeld or a similar attractor, then the bob-fly, or top dropper, of a slightly or totally buoyant kind which swims in the surface and creates some disturbance there to attract the trout's attention. The logic is simple and appears infallible, but in practice it is of an entirely different nature. The object is to fish the flies in the surface or within a few inches so that the trout which are cruising near the surface will see them and make an instinctive selection. In practice there are days when this principle works beyond the bounds of dreams and yet on other days one can cover trout rising all round but ignoring everything offered to them and the only thing to do is use common sense and trial and error based on observation.

The solution can sometimes be found by changing the attractor to the middle dropper; often, the patterns must be changed completely, and the usual method is to change the flies for patterns of smaller size. The speed of the retrieve, too, can be vital and it is usually possible to tell if this is so. If the trout are chasing your fly and not taking and the retrieve is slowed or speeded up on subsequent casts – and if there are enough fish for you to be able to assess their response – the results will be apparent. Usually, however, the solution is not so easy and the flies must come under scrutiny.

I never change the entire cast unless I am thoroughly dissatisfied with them. Experience will show which flies are the most successful for the individual and his particular style of fishing and he will be reluctant to change more than one of the flies at a time. Size and colour are important to trout, the speed of retrieve only triggers off their aggression if it is faster than that which they are used to and of a pattern which also has an effect on their reactions.

Trout 'prefer' to take their food lazily and if the fly you present to them resembles their food and appears edible and nutritious – and available – the chances are that that the trout will take it with confidence. This is the reason why so many takes occur as the flies are held in the water prior to being lifted for another cast. It is the prime art of shortlining which produces so many fish for the angler who can master the method.

Trout cruise in the upper layers of the water seeking food which has been blown on to it or is hatching on the surface and drifting along in the movement induced by current and wind action. This indicates that the less action a fly has the more natural it will appear if it is intended to resemble a struggling, hatching fly or a drowned one. The wake fly attracts because it imitates an insect skating on the surface or has been blown there, or is laying eggs.

The bob-fly, which is dapped before being recast, should be held in the surface film and away from the boat so that waves can wash round it, creating a wake of its own which must appear quite natural and highly attractive to the trout. At the same time the other flies on the cast will be sinking, having ceased their movements, and therefore also attractive to feeding fish. Obviously the fly on the surface is in view and can be seen if it is taken, but there will be no sign to the inexperienced eye if those beneath are taken.

If a trout takes on the surface, give it time to turn down with the fly before you strike and then if all is well it will be hooked. When the sunken fly is taken it is sometimes possible to detect the event as the leader makes a slight movement to left or right, even before a tug is felt. It is often the only warning and a strike should be made immediately any movement of the leader is seen, or if you see a boil and a flash of silver as the trout turns. All these are tell-tale signs that the fly has been taken.

I have found that fly presentation is easier in windy weather when I am using a weight-forward or long-belly line. However, if the wind is moderate a double-taper line is always preferable. There is only one criticism – and probably the only one – I make of the double-taper line, which is that it is not easy to change direction during a cast although it is not necessary that one should be able to do this. Sometimes, however, when fish are rising it helps to be able to present a fly in a different direction from straight down the wind, always assuming that one's partner has no objection.

When the angler is short-lining, fish location is very much the same as with any form of fly-fishing. It is safe to assume that there will always be trout feeding at the tail of the wind and providing that the wind is not too strong the fish will be found. A drogue is essential in a strong wind, and when other boats are present in a confined area it can be polite to use a drogue to keep the drift steady.

Every boat has some quirks in its drifting ability and again the drogue helps in straightening them out, most craft drifting away from their bows across the wind and in the bows an angler substantially heavier than his partner will help accentuate this drift. It is often essential that the boat should drift straight down-wind and it might be necessary to raise the outboard out of the water and fix the drogue at a point which compensates for the adverse angle, especially if the drift is wanted parallel to a bank or over a particular depth.

Left Jeanette Taylor with a fine 5 lb (2·25 kg) reservoir rainbow.
Below left Bob Church displays a superbly marked wild brown trout taken from Lough Mash, Co. Mayo.

As a rule, depth is crucial for success and the depth at which the trout will be depends, as always, on the time of year. It has already been said that there will always be fish on the leeward side of the water and this is particularly relevant in early season when the water has still to warm up. In fact, I never consider fishing anywhere else than on the leeward side early in the season. It means that drifts are often very short and the boat has to be well organised so that the drogue is pulled in and the motor started at the right time to give maximum fishing time on every drift.

During one flyfishing competition the wind was very strong and the fish were in an area along the leeward bank, which allowed a drift of only about 30 yards (3m), and it meant that the fishing was difficult and wet. But on the day there was nowhere else on the reservoir which would produce trout consistently and as it was a team event we were forced to put up with it all, which we did to good effect.

With regard to starting a drift after fishing one out, it should not be necessary to fish over *exactly* the same stretch of water twice running, and by not doing so the trout are rested and more water is covered. If a slightly different line is adopted at each drift the trout will probably stay on the feed all the time unless some carelessness causes them to move away. Should they do so, they can be located using some thought and thoroughness.

To quote an example, I was fishing the famous Grafham Water and my partner and I had located a shoal of brown trout in shallow water and they were obviously all close together. Another boat containing my friend and angling author Bob Church, driven by his partner and a boatman, approached us and we learned that they were not doing as well as us. I suggested that they divert round the shoal and drift close to the bank, but they motored straight over the shoal and on their first drift I noticed that the fish were farther out. I confirmed this on our next drift. Again the other boat went straight over the trout and they moved farther out still and by this time I had made it clear to Bob that the fish should be avoided when moving back up the wind and that the proper boatman ought to take over; the shoal had not only moved farther but had dispersed, and therefore contact with them was infrequent. This episode conclusively proved to me the effect of a motor on trout because we had been very careful and avoided them with very good results until the second boat arrived. But in the event it was of no consequence because we finished the eliminating round highly placed.

On long drifts the emphasis is not to use the motor because there is such a long while between them, but if the drift is along a bank the boat should be moved back up the wind well out. It is surprising how often fish can be found over deep water when there is nothing so far as one can see to hold them there, and on days when the trout do not respond to ordinary tactics it is sometimes very relaxing to set the boat up for a long drift and move right across the water in search of a few fish. I have made contact with some very large trout in this way.

LOCH-STYLE WITH SINKING LINE

A floating line is not synonymous with short-lining, in fact in early season, and at certain times when the fish prefer to lie deep, a fast-sinking line is absolutely essential. The problem with fishing a fast-sinking line when fishing in front of the boat is that if there is any appreciable rate of drift the boat catches up with the flies too quickly. There is nothing that can be done to prevent this happening. Nevertheless, the longer the cast that you can make, the more fishing time you will give yourself on each cast before the boat catches up.

When fishing with the sinking line I always choose water that is about 8ft (2.5m) deep, for I have had only limited success when fishing in water that was much shallower. The secret is to fish in water that allows you to cover the trout with a sinking line and if the drift takes you into shallower water there is no cause for concern because the odds are that the fish may be there too. In early season I have taken trout in water that was less than 2ft (0.5m) deep, and there were plenty of fish there, contrary to many people's expectations.

Having made a long cast, the next step is to do nothing other than keep up with the flies, which means a slow recovery but not one that affects the sinking of the line. It is surprising how often one gets takes on the drop while 'holding station' on the flies in this way and the knowing angler will always be prepared for it. The merest hint of a retrieve will not affect the sinking of the line and it might even be beneficial so far as the attraction of the flies is concerned. When they have sunk deep enough to be retrieved this should be made in a way that will not only keep up with the line but will also make the trout curious enough to investigate them. However, using a sinking line for a long time on a windy day is a very tiring method of flyfishing.

It is possible that trout will follow the fly for some distance and take it just before it is lifted from the water. If you see this happening, continue the retrieve until the line is pointing down and then smoothly lift the flies from the water; it is the moment when a long rod will prove its advantage. If possible, try to hold the bob fly briefly on the surface for takes often occur then so keep an eagle eye on the leader and the flies behind it. All the flies have been sunk, so it is a good idea to fish each one right to the surface and out of the water.

The length of the leader is not so important with a sinking line and I also think that contact with all the flies will be helped if there is a shorter distance between the end of the fly line and the bob. So far as the selection of flies to be fished on a sinking line is concerned it must be quite different from the choice made when a floating line is to be used. For example, in early season, when we are most likely to be using a sinking line, there will be no abundance of sedges or any other hatching insects, but daphnia will be about in numbers in early season, so by fishing an area where they have collected one can take trout consistently. The flies that do best here are white, flashy or coloured patterns. I also make up some glittery fry imitations which work very well while on the same cast I put a miniature Appetizer and equally small Viva. Even if the fry imitation does not get results I retain it because I know that it works well and it will either catch fish itself or it will attract the fish to one of the other flies on the line.

If I am not restricted on the size of fly I prefer moderately sized nymphs and fish them slowly. This lure can be very effective when fished on the sunk line, the most popular ones being Pheasant Tail of varying coloured thoraxes and the Ivens' Brown and Green Nymph. All these resemble fry in shape and the trout accept them either as that immature fish or as larvae.

A fast retrieve is also worth trying on occasion if the fish are not showing much interest. In my experience, although it does not happen very often, they will take a stripped fly after they have ignored a slow one.

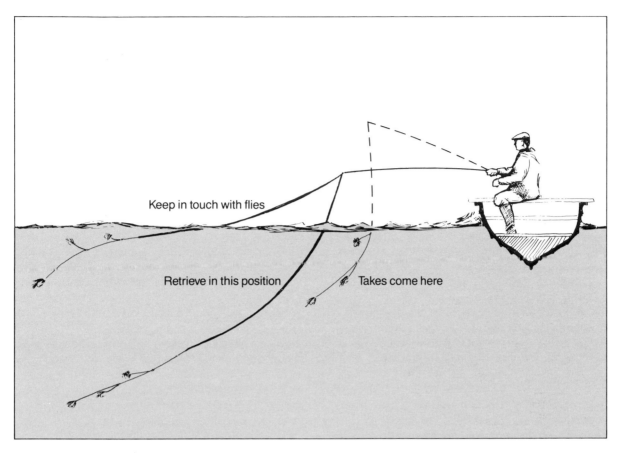

Keep in touch with flies

Retrieve in this position

Takes come here

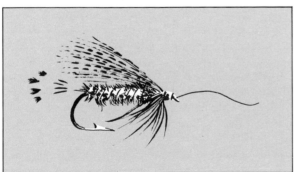

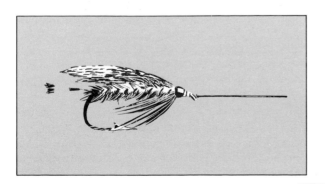

Above *Shortlining a sinking line: the flies will fish through the water and eventually be retrieved straight upwards. The retrieve should not start until the flies have sunk as deep as required.*
Left *A fly during a pause in the retrieve* (top), *and as it is retrieved* (lower).

COMPETITIVE FLYFISHING

The rules of these competitions depend on the organizers and the venue. In recent years there has been a massive upsurge in this kind of contest with the main events all being fished from boats and all using the short-lining method, used as a restriction. The anglers are allowed only to fish in front of the boat, casting behind is forbidden, with a boatman present as arbiter to ensure that the rules are adhered to.

The boat is permitted to drift only with the wind with both anglers fishing in front and if drogues are allowed they have to use the model supplied by the fishery. The aim is to make the event as even as possible so that individual skills in fish location and presentation have to be employed to get among the winners. The contests usually run from 10.00am-6.00pm, but in one important event, the Benson & Hedges International, some strange hours are imposed on the anglers which not only test one's fishing skill but also one's stamina.

These shortlining competitions are fun, but one does not have a choice of boat partner and while I have been fortunate I did on one occasion share a craft with an angler who did not enjoy his day and did little or nothing to make my day entertaining. But success makes any day enjoyable and one particular session stands out.

With a friend, Bev Perkins, I was fishing an English National eliminator on Grafham Water and between us we caught 52 trout, slightly less than twice the number of the nearest boat in the results. All the fish were caught in moderate conditions, with a floating line and small flies and the occasion was very enjoyable. These competitions are judged on weight of fish caught and not on numbers but we won with ease and I am not aware of more trout being taken in one boat in a similar contest.

To those trout fishermen who do not enter competitions and who may be wondering about limits on reservoirs, the answer is that a no-limit rule exists during the competitions and all the fish are given to charitable causes.

The nature of the contests means that stock fish of necessity must feature in the results if bags of any size are to be taken. Anglers who have located them should stay put and make the best of the situation. But it must be borne in mind that many stock fish appear to suffer from the 'soft' mouth syndrome and if they are treated roughly while being played one can tear the hook free. These trout must be played gently and eased to the net as, depending on the water, they do not show much energy.

There are other flyfishing competitions which rely on the rules of the water for their fishing technique, but these leave this kind of event wide open to the guile of those who will 'bend' the rules in order to win. Unfortunately it is not possible to supervise the kind of event where an individual is left alone to fish in whatever doubtful manner he can in order to win. Sadly, some individuals will go to the length of taking previously caught fish to the water, entering them as taken on the day. Behaviour of this kind is beyond the pale and I no longer take part in any event where this is a possibility.

ETIQUETTE

Extra care must be taken during competitions so that everyone competing will not be impeded, or that any infringements take place which interrupt their fishing. There are other sports which have the hindrance of opponents as part of the 'game' but in angling it is assumed that all those present are sportsmen who will allow fellow competitors to continue their efforts unimpeded. This applies particularly when returning to restart a drift, when fish should be left well alone and other anglers avoided, particularly downwind. In other words, treat the other anglers as you would have them treat you.

Top right *Two fishermen and a boatman drifting loch-style, strategically distanced from the bank, during a competition. In a competition, the methods allowed depend on the venue.*

Above *Anglers preparing for the off in a loch-style competition at Grafham Water, a reservoir which produces many fish in the 4–6 lb (1·8–2·7 kg) class and larger! The angler in the foreground has a thwartboard, yet to be positioned in the boat, which will provide him with greater comfort and increased height.*

91

FISHING SMALL STILLWATERS

Small stillwaters became very popular from the mid-1970s and since then the numbers have continued to increase. One such stillwater in the south of England yielded the British record rod-caught rainbow of 19lb 8oz (8.7kg) until it was beaten by a 21lb 4oz 4dr (9.6kg) trout from Scotland's Loch Awe in 1986 – and it is rumoured that there are even heavier rainbows swimming in more than one water in England.

Such waters are of a contentious nature in trout-fishing circles because they are usually stocked on a day-to-day basis, replacing every day those caught in order to maintain the same head of trout. These stock fish are 'green' and come to the fly readily, although there are still a few that have been hooked, broken away and become very wary. This happens once the trout have had the time to become acclimatized to the conditions in the water and have learned to seek food instead of it being given in pellet form.

This is a sweeping generalization which might suggest that small stillwater fish are easy, and available to be caught when an angler wants to boost his averages. But it is not the case and my friend Alan Pearson made the point in his book *Catching Big Trout*. He said that even after fishing waters holding huge rainbows I had never caught a double-figure trout. I readily own up! I have fished many stillwaters that hold these fish and my largest to date is a rainbow of exactly 9lb (4kg) from the famous Avington water in Hampshire. It was a resident female, lean and silver with a fully mended tail, and still had three other flies in its mouth. I was as pleased with that trout as I would have been with a dark-coloured, flabby fish with a stump of a tail and of much heavier weight.

For those unaware of the shortcomings of newly introduced trout, the tail is a giveaway. A trout is unable to fully grow its caudal (tail) fin in a stock pond because it will be rubbing its body against the sides of the enclosure and at the same time being nipped by the other fish. When released into open water it takes time for the tail to assume its natural appearance.

Another feature of stock fish can be a darker coloration and raw patches, usually around the jaws. The colouring is caused by stress due to the fish being moved into another environment. Another point about these trout is that they do not have the firmly muscled flesh that free-ranging fish develop while searching for and chasing food. The restricted space in a stewpond allows only for the trout to laze about and wait for the regular supply of food thrown in. Stock fish are force-fed on the pellets and when they have reached a good weight they are released into the fishery.

A free-ranging trout has to feed in order to survive and will grow only within the limitations of the food available in the water and the competition for it from other fish. Fortunately most small stillwaters were dug with this point in mind and food will have been taken into account at the planning stage.

One achievement of which I am particularly pleased is my introduction of mayfly to a small Northamptonshire lake which was dug on the farm of a friend, Roy Paterson. We planned and excavated this water and then put trout in it, introducing sticklebacks as food. One day while I was fishing the River Kennet in Berkshire there was a prolific hatch of mayfly, and making small air-holes in a plastic bag I collected as many male and females flies as I could and drove the eighty-odd miles to Roy's lake and released the mayfly into the bushes surrounding it. It was as simple as that and so far as I know there had been no mayfly anywhere in the area beforehand. However, two years later there occurred a mayfly hatch on the new water and it has happened ever since, making the lake a corner of nature on the farm and a very relaxing and satisfying place.

Some small waters, as do larger ones, have a natural mayfly hatch but this does not necessarily indicate that the fishing is easier. The trout will

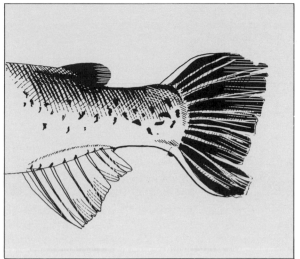

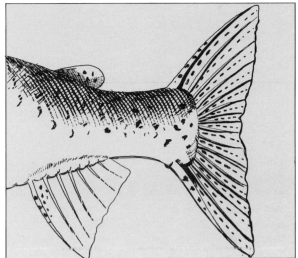

Above left *The tail fin of a newly stocked trout that has not recovered from its stewpond days.*
Above *A perfectly formed tail fin.*

readily rise to the hatched insects as they lay their eggs or lie spent on the surface, and very often they will feed happily on the nymphs as they emerge or swim through the water on their way to the surface.

Whether mayfly are present or not, the artificial Mayfly nymph is one of the best and deadliest flies on any small water. The fly was devised by the late Richard Walker, an angler who did a great deal for all kinds of fishing but who was particularly fond of stillwater trout fishing and his innovative thinking did much to further this branch of the sport in Britain.

On small waters, islands are features which must not be ignored and the sheltered side is the more attractive because it offers calm water in which surface food gathers. The margins of the island also provide a haven for fry and other kinds of natural food which trout eat. On the first visit the identification of feeding areas is often a matter of luck on small waters, but since it is usually possible to fish round the whole of the water comparatively quickly the fish can be located with the right fly and the correct method. A useful indication, too, is the sight of other ang-

lers, and whether they are catching fish or not tells you a lot about the area.

It is, then, a simple fact that the small stillwater can slot very nicely into the itinerary of the flyfisher. He can pay as little, or as much, as he pleases for his fishing and catch the type of fish that he prefers. He can choose the scenery, in most cases, that he prefers, and there is also the possibility of delicacy and finesse being needed to overthrow the larger specimens. Some small stillwaters have a stream fishery running alongside them which provides an added challenge, especially if it is a chalk stream.

The features found in small stillwaters, such as deep water, shallow reaches, islands and inlets, all add to the 'curiosity' value and charm of a particular water. And with the number of them that abound, the small stillwaters have most definitely made a niche for themselves which they will keep indefinitely.

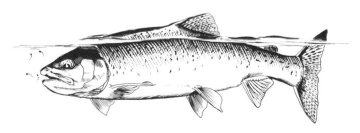

TACKLE

The kind of tackle required on the average small water is a rod of maximum length of 9ft (2.7m) or 9ft 6in (2.9m) because long casting is not usually desirable due to the possibility of lining the fish. The shorter rod is an advantage because the trout tend to cruise along the edges of the water and so one can fish right to the bank and my Farlow's 6ft (1.8m) 'Midge' has been used with success on many small waters of this kind. This rod is made of split-cane and weights under 2oz (56gr) and the best trout I have caught with it was 8lb 8oz (3.8kg) and it dwarfed the rod!

A lightweight floating line is preferable, or a very slow sinker, and I like a double-taper because of the more delicate presentation it allows the angler. Here, it must be remembered that the majority of small waters are quite clear and although this enables the trout to see the fly from farther away it also makes the angler more easily visible. Any shortcomings in the tackle and its presentation will therefore stand out alarmingly. Vibrations from one's movement on the bank will more easily be transmitted to the fish and so stealth is particularly essential because one is nearer to the fish and every action must be made quietly.

Fast-sinking lines are an advantage on those waters which are sufficiently large to have deep areas which can be fished with a long cast. Most small waters also have deep areas but they do not have the room to allow a long cast, being more like 'craters' on the bottom and these have to be fished with a leaded fly and a long leader.

Again, clarity plays a part on the length of the leader, for I believe that it is beneficial to fish with the longest leader possible, particularly when the trout have the opportunity of inspecting the tackle. Of course, a long leader is sometimes impossible to use because of the prevailing wind, but most small waters allow the use of single flies only and in rough conditions to be forced to fish this way is a real advantage. A wind is always helpful because it makes for concealment of the angler and diffuses the disturbance made by the entry of the fly into the water.

Sometimes, fish are attracted by the plopping of a leaded fly as it enters the water and when casting in the proximity of a fish there is the chance either of alerting it, or of attracting it. Individual trout tend to frequent the same territory until they are caught or harassed into moving away. Usually, when a poor cast has alarmed a fish, resting it results in it returning a little later to take up station once more. However, the trout will be more wary than before and it will treat any more bad casts by leaving the area in a hurry. It will even move away fast from a reasonable cast and you will not have many chances of success with this fish. So, assume that all trout in the vicinity are 'educated' and treat them accordingly.

Below *Contemplating the flat calm conditions at Bayham Abbey, Kent.*
Right *Battling amongst the weeds against a lively trout. His adequate tackle allows this angler to keep the fish's head up.*

TACTICS

One can often observe trout rising in the same place, or cruising along the bank. If the rises take the form of a swirl the fish is likely to be feeding just below the surface, so an unweighted fly should be offered it; a nymph pattern such as a Gold Ribbed Hare's Ear would be ideal. The cast should be made beyond the fish so that it rose last between the end of the fly line and where the fly has landed, then a slow retrieve should be made.

This is where the importance of a long leader shows, for the main line causes the most disturbance. Repeated casts are advisable because the trout is likely to remain in the area and if it doesn't another will come along. Here is one of the advantages of maintaining a high stocking policy in a confined water, but it may be that some areas of a stillwater will not hold fish and it is very apparent on all the waters I have fished that some parts fish infinitely better than others.

Small stillwater trout do not show the same aggression as do fish in larger waters and rivers, and ripping an attractor fly or lure through them does not work. These artificials do take fish but not if they are fished in the same way as they would be on a large open water where they would be successful.

Another quality peculiar to small stillwater trout is their readiness to rise to a dry fly and it is possible to catch these at all times of the year. Perhaps it is because they are conditioned to finding their food on the surface in the form of pellets or anything floating that arouses their interest. Another reason might be that the head of trout in the water forces the fish to eat a wider variety of things than trout in a larger habitat. But whatever the reason, it has been proved to me by fishery owners and managers that stock-trout that have been in a water for a longish period will still immediately rise to pellets that are thrown into the water.

Rises to a dry fly on a small stillwater are usually done quite lazily, the trout slowly tilts and swirls at the fly, then after taking it turns gently down and away. If there is a fast rise it is because of competition between the fish, making them snatch at it. It is very easy to see how long to give the trout before striking, for the speed of the rise will be a direct indication. In these waters the trout are usually cruising slowly about for there is little or no current to hold them in line while feeding and most have a large enough surface area to cause them to be seriously affected by the wind, particularly during periods of colder weather.

Some small lakes remain open all the year round but this is not always the case. The rainbow trout is not indigenous to the British Isles, so it is possible to fish for it throughout the year if the fishery owner is willing to work without a break.

Present the fly to the front of the fish and allow time for it to settle.

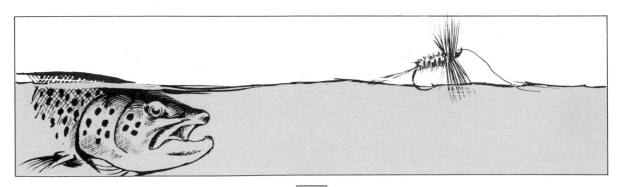

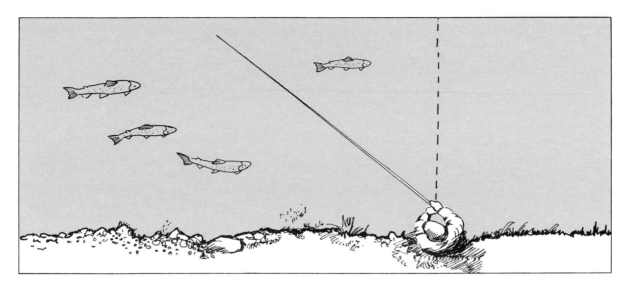

A cast made at an angle to the bank gives cruising fish a long sight of the fly, and produces an unusual retrieve.

Some of the larger reservoirs allow fishing for rainbows right through to the end of the year, but their by-laws insist that all brown trout must be returned unharmed to the water. It is interesting to note here that since this innovation some very large specimen trout have been taken whose weights have not been equalled during the legitimate open season for the species. While some small waters remain open for rainbow trout fishing, a number of fisheries also stock brown trout and it has become fashionable to introduce very large specimens weighing into double-figures.

Brown trout in small waters tend to be territorial-minded and pugnacious, taking up residence in one particular area. They are also wary and will follow a fly for a long way and often for a number of times before shying off. The essential ingredient for taking one of these large fish is a good presentation allied to skill and good fortune, but they must be caught in the first few well-placed casts. If there is no result it is best to move on.

In fact, the best way of fishing any small water is to keep on the move, pausing regularly to look for any signs of moving or feeding fish, but their presence is not always obvious. This is where polarized glasses come into their own. These cut through the surface reflections and enable you to see what is going on beneath the surface for only

then can you distinguish any fish cruising about below. The two points to remember when you see fish in these waters are that they are larger than they appear to be and are certainly deeper than you think.

The only way to take these fish is with the weighted fly and it must be presented with inch-perfect accuracy, for the fish will not deviate from their paths if the fly is not directly in front of their heads. Neither will they take any fly that is being pulled towards them, i.e. moving in the opposite direction. I found this out the hard way when fishing small waters before I realized why I was not getting them.

These fish, however, will take a fly that is being pulled away from them and will even deviate from their course if the fly is close enough and appears to be fleeing. It is, of course, the induced-take principle again.

Stealth, confidence, patience and skill – all are needed to stalk and catch such trout, as well as a fly that is sunk to the correct depth, although I am not in favour of one that sinks too quickly because it hampers presentation, a matter that can have disastrous consequences when you put it right in front of the trout. I have seen a fish inspect a fly only to shy away when the fly suddenly sinks back towards it. Trout are conditioned to take food fleeing away, not moving towards them.

A cruising trout that has been seen will return along the same path. They make continual journeys in the same area and it is possible to time them so that the fly is presented at the moment when they next appear. Here, it is preferable to

have the fly at a lower level than the fish so that it can be raised as the fish approaches. This is easier than getting the fly to sink to the right level at the correct moment.

If you feel that the trout will come from the left, the cast should be made to the left so that the fly will be moving with the trout following and able to see it. Theoretically, if you have got it all right there is every chance that the trout will take the fly. If it does, and you strike too early, you will have ruined the whole achievement.

Even if the trout is nothing but a shadowy 'something' the white of the mouth will be visible and once that has closed on the fly and the fish has turned the strike can be made. On many occasions the trout will pause with its mouth not properly closed on the fly, and a strike then will merely prick the fish or miss it altogether.

It is also easy to be too slow on the strike. Trout can eject a fly extremely fast, much more quickly than an angler can react, so it is essential to have a degree of anticipation – but not too much. In some respects, when the fish takes the fly it might be better not to have it in sight at all, but that really is taking the gilt off the gingerbread.

Many anglers fish small waters 'blindly', but in all fairness there are many places where it is not possible to stalk the fish, so the style is dictated by the water. Where bank space is restricted there are usually very many artificials in the water through the season and the trout have seen them all being fished and retrieved in the same way. On some hard-fished waters there are many anglers fishing at the same time, so if you can offer the fly in a different way to that which they are, there is more chance of hooking them. I also think that since trout stay close to the bank a fly retrieved along it, rather than at right angles, will have a better chance of success.

In the winter, trout congregate in the deepest part of the water on the leeward side of the fishery, and a floating line with a weighted fly that is swung round a corner will produce results every time. At this time of year I use a dark fly and one with some marabou in the dressing is often very successful. I do not like lead-headed flies even though they are popular and successful because I do not enjoy casting with them.

Under crowded conditions such as these, a powerful rod helps an angler to cast a greater distance, thereby giving him an advantage in reaching the fish.

PLAYING A FISH

I have included this section in small stillwaters because I have found that many more features are likely to exist in these waters than in other types. It is the comparatively deep nature of most small stillwaters that give the trout something of an advantage. And it is unlikely that a strong, running fish could round an island on a large water as he might do in so many small waters. There are many other anomalies on small waters unlikely to be found on larger ones.

Let us consider how to act when a trout is hooked. Richard Walker said that it is well to lower one's profile when playing a fish so that it would not be alarmed when it was drawn to the net. Surely, a hooked fish is alarmed already, but I agree with Walker for a different reason. Anyone who has played a trout will know that unless it is a large specimen it is usually easy to turn a fish that has run a distance and bring it back to the net. But it is much more difficult to influence the actions of a fresh fish when it is close to the rod, because the fish naturally resists all attempts to bring it up through the water. It keeps its head down and away from the direction of the pull of the line. Brown trout are very stubborn at this time and can take a long while to net once they have their heads down.

The answer is to exert sidestrain, which throws the fish off-balance and makes it easier to control. So, unless the trout is under the rod-tip, by maintaining a low profile the angle of the pull of the line is more to one side, making the fish use more energy in taking line. A short rod also has the effect of reducing the line angle.

Sidestrain is a way of changing the direction of pull and can be used when a largish fish has its head down and its tail up and proving difficult to control. It is done by breaking the wrist to left or right and the change of line angle has the effect of making the fish deviate from the direction it wants to swim and ultimately tiring it to the point when it can be netted.

An angler can also apply sidestrain to a freshly hooked fish that is thrashing about on the surface. It might be spectacular, but it is not desirable to allow a fish to behave in this way because every lunge and shake of the trout's head may be weakening the hook-hold. The action to take is to drop the rod to the side and level with the water and apply sidestrain and in my experience when this is done the fish immediately swims deeper. All trout, of all sizes, that I have applied this method to has responded in the way I have described. The only fish which did not react in this way was a 30lb (13.5kg) fresh-run salmon I had hooked on a Size 10 fly on the River Tweed, but that is a different story!

Floating algae is another problem which I have encountered when fishing small waters. This green slime collects on the surface in blankets and trout will shelter beneath it. It is best to fish around the edge of the weed, where it is not very thick. If algae is clinging to the line, the rod-tip can be dipped into the water and the fish played from there until it is back into open water. It is in fact another way of applying sidestrain.

Never allow algae to collect on the line because it cannot be removed while you play the fish and adds so much weight to the line that direct contact with the trout is impossible. If the fish is not securely hooked there is a very good chance of it being lost, especially if it is a large specimen.

There are a number of ways in which a trout can behave when hooked so it is impossible to predict what will happen. All one can say is that a fish hooked at the surface will usually thrash on the surface before making its first move in the fight. This is a crucial time because the hook is most likely to pull free from a thrashing fish.

The fish's initial reaction will depend on the type of take. If the fish has hooked itself by taking the fly at speed, it is likely to continue on a run for as long as it has the strength against the tackle being used.

If the take has been in the form of the line drawing tight with the angler striking to set the

hook, the fish is more likely to hold station for a moment before it settles into the fight. Very often this results in the fish shaking its head, and it is vital to keep the pressure on the fish, with the rod raised high, in order that the hook sets firm. A large fish usually takes in this way, and it really sets the adrenalin racing to realize that what is at the other end of the fly-line is not going to budge easily.

Whenever a trout has its head down in a direct pull against the rod, the pressure on the hook-hold is increased, therefore increasing the danger of the hook tearing free before the fish is netted. The rod must be held so that it is at right angles to the fish (the line leaves the tip-ring at right angles to the rod), otherwise the rod will not absorb sufficient strain, and the fish will then have more of a direct pull to the angler's hand. This increases the weight of the pull, making the hook-hold precarious.

If the rod is held to one side, this will not have a detrimental effect so long as a good angle is maintained to the fish. This is important because sidestrain is the most important ally we have in the repertoire of moves when playing a lively and strong trout. It can be summed up quite simply, I think, by the following easy pointers:

□ If a trout thrashes on the surface whilst

The use of sidestrain is the best way to fight a fish in water where it has plenty of cover.

hooked, apply sidestrain.

□ If a trout is running for an obstacle, apply sidestrain.

□ If a trout is looking as if it will run a long distance, apply sidestrain. If it has taken a lot of line already, walk along the bank to increase the effectiveness of the sidestrain.

□ If a trout has its head down whilst being fairly well under the rod tip, apply sidestrain to turn its head in a different direction.

□ If a trout is twisting and thrashing beneath the surface, apply sidestrain to cause it to stop its acrobatics.

□ If a trout leaps from the water, give it an amount of slack immediately, and when the line tightens again apply sidestrain to keep it down in the water.

There is no need to use brute force against a fish. It would not be sporting in any event to use tackle which would allow this, but it is easy to gauge just how much force is required. There are times when a trout is so strong that one can only hold onto the rod and hope, but even then one must remain calm in order to seize any opportunity to take the advantage.

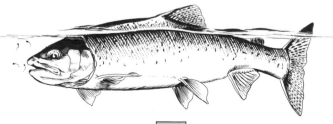

SEASONAL CHANGES

It may be obvious that the water begins to warm up as spring progresses into summer, but the effect that this has on the fish is not always as obvious. It is a fact that more trout activity, in the form of rises, will be evident on most days. The reason for this is that the aquatic insect life has exploded and is now ranging throughout the water, with nymphs and larvae transforming and becoming adult flies as they ascend through the water to the surface. Whereas in the very early season the trout found more food on the bed of the water, they can now find sufficient at the surface most of the time, and so trout will be feeding both at the surface and on the bottom. The larger cannibalistic trout, which only sometimes take an insect, will also be present.

There is another factor, often overlooked: the fish are now reasonably well educated, due to the season having been under way for some time, and the trout will have seen many fly patterns that make no attempt to imitate their natural food. This does not necessarily apply to recently introduced stock fish in a water with a regular stocking pattern, but these are generally smaller fish. The prize catch is a large over-wintered trout, and if these can be taken on an imitative pattern then the sporting value of the achievement is enhanced manyfold. It is also true that the pressure put on the water by large numbers of anglers will probably have increased due to the warmer weather conditions and the pleasure of casting to rising fish.

In early season the coloured water which is often prevalent, and the low light conditions, mean that a larger, abstract type of fly can be successful, whereas when the water clears and the light is brighter, a small fly will stand a better chance of success. This will be increased further if that fly actually imitates the trout's natural food well. It will almost certainly produce better results if it is fished slowly, and if results are not forthcoming the fly size should be scaled down, time and time again if necessary – particularly in bright conditions where the water is very clear. If the trout are at the same depth as the fly, they will seize it eventually and are more likely to do so if it is the same size as the natural or smaller, but will usually avoid it if it is larger. When I first started my trout fishing, I thought it logical that if I presented the trout with a large version of the fly they were taking, I would assuredly catch fish. I quickly learned that this line of thinking is totally erroneous. It is possible that the trout will happily suck in all offerings within reach and remain casually doing so for as long as the hatch prevails, but if something out of the ordinary looms into view it will 'wake him up' and cause him to view it with suspicion rather than greed.

I would consider a very long leader to be essential, and unless I am shortlining from a boat I would use only one dropper. The reason for this is that the flies are in the water for a longer period of time, and more flies might cause the cast to sink below the required level. In addition, a number of different patterns on the same cast might not produce the desired natural effect.

On certain occasions it can be beneficial to use a sink-tip line or one with a very slow sinking rate, such times as when there should be a hatch but there is none in evidence, and you suspect that the fish are feeding just a few feet beneath the surface. Such conditions are induced by warm weather suddenly changing to slightly cooler. The emerging fly is then reluctant to fight through a layer of colder water at the surface, and in effect becomes 'trapped' and nomadic. The trout will still feed on these, but will not be seen to be doing so. It will be necessary to test the fishing depth until the fish are located.

An angler carries away his prize rainbow.

FLIES FOR STILLWATER FISHING

Most of my trout fishing has been conducted in the stillwaters of the Midland areas of England. These waters are visited by large numbers of anglers and because I fish them regularly I have been more innovative with the flies I have tied, especially the lures and attractor artificials because others of the more traditional patterns have worked successfully for decades.

On occasion someone has some success with a slightly new twist to one of the established patterns but generally I prefer to hold with tradition with the imitative patterns and wet flies, leaving my experiments for the lures.

I do not feel it necessary to carry every pattern in my fly box, even if that were possible, and a good spread of sizes and colours is all that is necessary. With lures, wings of different lengths and materials make the fishing interesting and thought-provoking.

Hooks

This section is pertinent to all types of fly-fishing.

I am indebted to Alan Bramley of Partridge of Redditch for the ideas which have stood me in such good stead with some of my fly-tying innovations. Not only has he increased my knowledge of hook-making procedures and characteristics with his advice and a fascinating tour around the factory, but he has also introduced me to some ideas from the USA, for whose fly-tyers and fishers I have the utmost respect.

The Partridge hooks are hand-made, and the art of making them has to be seen to be truly appreciated. The main feature that I am drawn to on Partridge hooks is the relatively short point and small barb. On hooks such as the Bucktail Streamer (for lures) and the Captain Hamilton (for nymphs and wet flies), I prefer the nice wide gape and round bend. The Captain Hamilton is particularly good for buzzers and shrimps, for example, where the dressing intrudes into the bend of the hook, yet the gape is still sufficiently wide that the hooking quality is not impaired.

The hook is just as integral a part of the flyfisher's equipment as anything else. In small flies the gape of the hook and the weight of the wire used can be critical. The gape affects the tying possibilities and the hooking potential, whereas the weight of the wire affects the way in which the fly fishes. The Captain Hamilton, for instance, is available in fine wire, medium wire and heavy wire and the choice is left to the tyer's preference. The fine wire is obviously the right choice for dry flies, the medium for wet flies and the heavy for nymphs. But there are permutations; for instance, a wet fly tied on fine wire will fish higher in the water, as will a nymph, and if a wet fly needs to be fished lower in the water (so that it stays down when fished reasonably fast) it can be tied on heavy wire.

There are numerous other hooks to which Alan introduced me. The Swedish Dry Fly is especially designed for the easy tying of a parachute hackle on dry flies, and the grub hooks and sedge hooks have arched shanks giving the nymphs tied on them a hump-backed appearance. These different types of hooks are well worth investing in by the imaginative fly-tyer, because it is always very satisfying to create a fly which looks good and subsequently proves to be effective at catching fish.

In the case of lures, it is not necessary to take the weight of the hook into account. The only hook that I like to avoid is the lure hook that has a straight eye. I prefer all of my flies to have a good 'down eye' so that I can tie a turl knot. Having said this, though, I would add that I do prefer the straight-eyed hook as the second one in a tandem dressing.

Taking everything into consideration, for any flyfisher who ties his own flies, I cannot recommend strongly enough the importance of experimenting with a wide range of different hooks.

Lures and wet flies for stillwater fishing.

NYMPHS

Buzzer Nymphs

There is little that can be added to what has already been written about these chironomid imitations. The larva of the chironomid is the blood-worm and the Buzzer Nymph is an imitation of the pupa stage of the adult insect. There are many different versions, all from superlative fly-tiers, and they catch fish. My preference is a small, simple pattern which will float in or just beneath the surface film, so fine wire hooks are essential.

Chironomids (also known as midges) pupate in the early stages and the adult flies come in different colours. The more popular colour of the Buzzer Nymph is black, but they can be red, ginger, brown or green and a cast of nymphs with various colours might make the difference when there is no apparent hatch.

I do not tie the 'Suspender' Buzzer popularized by John Goddard. My flies are either straightforward or have a loop of feather fibre over the thorax to present an emerging effect. The body should be in the appropriate colour silk, ribbed with fine silver wire. The thorax is peacock or ostrich herl and a few white fibres at the head and tail suggest the breathing tubes of the natural. This fly must be fished with barely any movement. I have taken many trout on a slow-sinking line with Buzzers in early season.

Pheasant-tail Nymphs

There are two basic ways of tying this Nymph – with a tail or without one. The tail-less dressing is the one popularized by Arthur Cove, the acknowledged stillwater Nymph angler. This is a versatile fly that can be tied in a range of sizes and with different coloured thoraxes.

The construction of the body is three or four fibres from the centre tail feather of a cock pheasant wound round the hook to the thorax, which is then formed either with more fibres or seal's fur or silk. On my Nymphs the thorax is then given a shell-back by pulling loose fibres over it and securing them at the head. Throat hackle or fibres are optional. This fly can resemble a wide range of naturals and can be fished extra fast or slow.

Amber Nymph

This is tied in exactly the same way as the Claret Nymph, in small sizes. It resembles the pupa of the sedge fly and in a weighted version will take trout in deep water.

Shrimp

This fly works on any waters and all the ones I tie are weighted to varying degrees and in small sizes. The weight is provided by lead strips secured on the back of the hook and the body is dubbed seal's fur ribbed with gold. Amber or orange versions are both successful. The hackle is furnace cock palmered the length of the body and secured at butt and head, and a few can be left protruding from the butt to form a tail, but only stubs, not a full tail. The hackle is then trimmed on the back right to the body to produce the effect of legs. It is fished on its back, slowly along the bottom. This pattern is exactly as Richard Walker described it and it has caught a great many trout for me under all conditions.

Bloodworm

This is a pattern shown to me by an angler who was extraordinarily successful on a dour day on Rutland Water, but to my regret I do not know his name. It is a simple dressing, the tail and body are of red marabou substitute and the body is ribbed with fine silver wire or tinsel. The very small head is painted red and hook sizes are small. This will take fish as it sinks and also if it is left swinging with the line. The less this fly is moved the better it performs.

A large rainbow trout with the tackle on which it was caught.

Black-and-Peacock Spider

A simple fly which consists of a body of peacock herl and a spun black hen hackle at the head. I have versions which are slightly weighted for fishing small waters, but on reservoirs where there is more wind this fly is best left to drift. It also has produced many trout in early season on a slow-sinking line.

Claret Nymph

Again, a simple tying and on its day one that proves infallible. The body is claret seal's fur ribbed with gold and with a pheasant-tail fibre shell-back. The throat fibres are also pheasant tail. This fly is best fished just under or in the surface film and barely moved. Sizes are small.

Mayfly Nymph

Again, this is a pattern created for flyfishermen by Richard Walker. It is an involved tying but will catch fish on any water, even where there are no natural mayflies. It is usually weighted and is most popular on small stillwaters. The tail is composed of three cock pheasant tail fibres and the body of angora wool ribbed with brown tying silk. The thorax is picked out along the sides with a needle and has a shell-back of cock pheasant fibres; the head is clear-varnished brown silk.

These are but a tiny proportion of the nymph patterns available but to me they cover virtually every shape that is likely to be met by trout while feeding on natural nymphs and larvae. I have omitted many patterns such as Ivens' Brown-and-Green Nymph, the Stick Fly, and so on but their silhouette to the fish is shown by one of the patterns I have included here and I leave it to the angler as to whether he wishes to extend his collection of flies to a huge degree. I remain convinced that size, shape and movement are the main criteria for deceiving the trout, and colour is secondary even though trout can distinguish colours.

Kingford Killer

This pattern, as far as I know, hails from Devon and was shown to me years ago by an old friend, John Evans. This fly was named after a Devon village and is successful in that area. I have caught many fish on the pattern and its variations in reservoirs, lakes and streams. Its most attractive feature is the use of deer hair, which shows up very well in the water.

It can be tied either with or without a tail. A few fibres of long deer hair are plucked and tied in at the bend of the hook, then twisted into a rope and wound around the hook up to the thorax, which is then formed by more turns of the deer, which is then tied off at the eye. On the original version there is a silver rib and a small black wing. I have dispensed with the wing on my own patterns, and the incorporation of lead foil as an underbody makes a very effective small stillwater fly. A thorax of differing colours is useful to have to hand, and I tie it in a grub shape and in a pheasant-tail nymph shape. Both are equally successful.

Stick Fly

In its original form, this is a very uninteresting fly but is, nevertheless, a killing pattern with a high success rate. The original pattern is tied on a long-shank hook, with a body of peacock herl ribbed with copper wire as far as the thorax; the thorax is formed with pale tying silk and a sparse-spun brown hackle behind the eye of the hook. The attractiveness of the pattern (to the angler at least) is enhanced by the addition of a green or red tag for the tail, and even a brighter thorax. It is the basic shape and the 'fuzzy' outline of the fly caused by the herl which, I am sure, is the reason for its success. It is fished slowly.

Damselfly Nymph

This is another pattern which can be tied in various colours and is open to much experimentation as long as the basic nymph shape remains unaltered.

Although the damselfly is not in evidence until high summer, this nymph pattern works well throughout the year, and although most users advocate that it should be fished quickly, in darting fashion, I have also caught many fish by fishing it very slowly, and inching back either deep or sub-surface.

The underbody can be leaded or not. When leaded it is a popular fly on small stillwaters. The body is made from seal fur and can be light green or dark green, or a mixture. The thorax is formed by the use of the same material, and wing-cases are added by pulling pheasant tail fibres over the thorax. The tail is also tied with pheasant tail fibres. The hackle is made from spun partridge hackles, and generally there is no rib. I have seen successful patterns which added a green or yellow tag for the tail.

This is a large nymph which is usually tied on long-shank hooks of size 8 or 10.

Green Pea

This fly is credited to Arthur Smith, an Oxford tackle dealer I knew when I first started trout fishing, and is one that I had shamefully forgotten until reminded of it recently. It is a very effective fly when fished on a floating line. The hook length is divided into thirds. The front and rear third consist of lime-green ostrich herl, and the middle third fluorescent red wool. The whole is ribbed with fine silver wire. Hook sizes are small, I usually use a size 14 long-shank or smaller.

Montana Nymph

I first discovered this fly in the late Joe Brooks's book, *Trout Fishing*, in the early 1970s and I tied up the pattern faithfully to good effect. It has recently become popular in Britain with numerous different coloured thoraxes. It is tied on a small long-shank hook with a body of black chenille and black cock hackle tail. The thorax is yellow with palmered black cock hackle legs, and a black shell-back of chenille. There is no ribbing in the Joe Brooks dressing. Fished deep and slow it is deadly.

When tying nymphs, it is always worth experimenting in a calculated way. Even with nymphs, the addition of a red or green tag or thorax, or some other part of the fly, can make all the difference to its effectiveness.

There is also the question of buoyancy, which can affect the effectiveness of a fly. The addition of deer hair, or a buoyant underbody of cork or polystyrene, can often cause the fly to fish high in the water so that it attracts trout. This, of course, gives the opposite effect to leading the underbody in order to cause it to fish deeper.

I have experimented with deer hair to good effect on many nymphs. As well as giving buoyancy to a nymph, spun white deer hair also gives it the added advantage of visibility. It is as well to be prepared for the days when it is necessary to hunt through the entire fly box in order to find a killing pattern. If one has something unusual or different to hand on those days, it might increase the chance of success. I do, though, always adhere to the basic nymph shape so that the trout will not think that something too strange is going on.

As well as the traditional patterns, I have tied some successful ones from my own ideas, and I have also come across some local patterns which have proved to be very effective.

I have seen some weird and wonderful creations, such as a Daphnia Fly made from knotted monofilament tied to a hook! The thought and application given to this fly impressed me. However, trout do not take individual Daphnia, but have to be aggravated into taking other food when they are so engrossed.

WET FLIES

Dunkeld

A well-established and traditional pattern and one that I always include on my cast at the start of the day, either on the point or in the middle. This is essentially an attractor although it makes use of materials which are used in imitative patterns. The tail is golden pheasant fibres and the body gold, flat tinsel or mylar; ribbing the fly with gold wire helps to resist the attacks made upon the body material by the teeth of trout. The wings are bronze mallard fibres (I roll mine rather than pair them up) and the throat hackles are hot orange cock fibres. Jungle cock is optional and looks good but I am not certain that trout prefer them. Mine are dressed on a heavy wire hook to take the fly down in the water and hold it there, sinking the cast and providing an anchorage for the forward flies. Hook sizes are small. All the flies I recommend as wet flies are tied on normal-shank hooks, size 10, 12 or 14.

Mallard and Claret

Another traditional fly and quite buoyant because of the body material. It takes trout all the year round and is one of the best wet flies you can have. The body is claret seal's fur ribbed with gold wire, the tail is golden pheasant tippets and the throat hackle black cock; wings are bronze mallard.

Soldier Palmer

It has been said before that this must be the most popular fly currently in use. It is fished on the bob-fly position and dibbled in the surface as far as possible. It represents a hatching chironomid bursting into the air in a flash of colour. The body is red seal's fur ribbed with gold, the tail either natural red cock hackle or fluorescent red wool in moderation. The body is palmered natural red cock hackle and another is palmered at the head. A tip: when palmering, use two hackles wound in opposite directions. If one only is used the direction of the hackle fibres gives a propeller-like effect leading to the cast or dropper length being kinked. With two hackles, in opposite directions, they cancel out the tendency to spin in the air.

Bloody Butcher

Another traditional pattern and an attractor to be fished on the point or middle. The tail is red ibis substitute and the body silver tinsel or mylar. Red cock forms the throat hackle and the wings are mallard wing in purple or dark blue.

Watson's Fancy

A traditional pattern with which I have caught trout over many years. The tail is golden pheasant tippets and the body red silk at the butt and black silk forward, both ribbed with silver wire. The hackle is black cock, the wing of black crow or similar. Traditionally this dressing has jungle cock eyes. For me, this fly seems to work better in dull, cool weather.

Silver Invicta

This is a sedge pattern although it is also an attractor which works exceedingly well. The body is tinsel but it fishes high in the water because of its palmered hackle. The tail is golden pheasant and the body silver tinsel or mylar with a palmered furnace hackle secured at head and butt. The throat hackle is blue jay and the wing centre hen pheasant tail, although it works equally well with bronze mallard. Again, ribbing the body with round tinsel gives some protection from teeth, especially in preserving the palmered

A landed fish is best held in the net.

hackle. I prefer this fly to the Dunkeld on dull days and tying it on a heavy wire hook combats the buoyancy of the hackle, but it is more of a 'planing' effect than buoyancy.

Greenwell's Glory

A pattern for my box which can be tied with or without a tail. The tail, if decided upon, is yellow cock fibres, with the body of primrose wool or floss ribbed with gold wire and the wing is starling. The throat hackle is badger cock hackle. It is fished in the middle of the cast.

Grenadier

Another very successful fly, basically a Soldier Palmer but tied with orange instead of red seal's fur. It is fished on the bob-fly.

Light-coloured Sedge

A recent discovery of mine and one which has become a firm favourite. The body is buff seal's fur or something similar, with a palmered natural brown cock hackle and a wing of hen pheasant tail. There is no tail or throat hackle. This fly does well for me when fished in the middle of the cast.

Murraghs

I watched Robert McHaffie, a superb fly-dresser from Northern Ireland, tie this pattern and then experimented with it myself with good results. I use olive green, claret or grey seal's fur for the body which is then palmered with furnace cock hackle and ribbed with gold or silver wire (I prefer gold). There is an over-wing of bronze mallard or hen pheasant tail, depending upon whether a dark or light fly is required, then I spin a furnace cock hackle forward of the wing. There is no tail or throat hackle and this fly works superbly as a wake fly. Fished dry, it has caught many trout, often taken as it alights on the water. I fish it as a bob-fly.

Red Tag

A simple fly but one that has taken many trout for me. The tail is a red woollen tag and the body is black floss silk ribbed with silver. The hackle is spun black cock hackle at the head. It is fished as the bob-fly and when dibbled in the surface is infallible on the right day.

Muddler Minnow

As far as I know, this pattern is the same as the American original as tied by Don Gapen. The body is gold tinsel and the tail and wing of oak turkey wing. The head is formed by spinning natural deer hair from about a quarter of the length of the hook shank to the eye and then clipping it to shape. I fish it as a wake fly when the weather is dull, usually later in the season when the sedges can be seen skating on the surface.

Again, I do not pretend that the above-named flies are all that anyone might need, but they are the patterns which I use most of all, and can be supplemented by many others which I turn to if the first selections are not bringing trout to the net.

This is an area of flyfishing which has been improved in recent years, but the majority of fish are still taken on the favoured traditional patterns. Some patterns are 'improved' by the use of coloured tags or flashy material in the wings, but in the main I prefer to keep my wet flies simple and, for a change, conventional. When trout are feeding high in the water they are looking for specific food and the size, colour and shape are of paramount importance, allied to the depth of fishing and the speed of retrieve. I do not believe that a coloured tag or flashy wing will attract a fish and cause it to rise in the water, or travel any distance to take that fly in preference to natural food. The use of colour in Dunkelds and Invictas, for example, is more subtle and does not glare so obviously at a fish as unnatural fluorescents. A fluorescent is useful, however, when it comes to fishing wet flies at depth.

I have tried the bright fly theory many times during competition fishing, and the only regular success I have achieved with bright colours is with the straightforward hot orange, which can be very useful when there is an abundance of stock fish in the area and one needs to make up numbers. All the better trout that I have taken (and many which I have lost!) have come to a traditional pattern. However, it is worth experimenting with wet flies by varying patterns slightly or by adding deer hair or similar material for extra buoyancy.

When fishing the wet fly, it is important to remember that the higher the wave on the water, the larger the fly size can be, but still taking into account the brightness and water clarity. When there is a substantial wave on the water, I always use a bob-fly with plenty of hackles and buoyancy so that it makes a real impression. On a dull day this can provide very exciting fishing indeed. It is better to use a long rod so that the flies can be held as high in the water as possible. The advantage of a windy day is that the flies can be held almost stationary in the water while the waves wash around them, keeping them high and moving.

The bob-fly is perhaps the most important fly on the cast because it is often the one that attracts the fish. I have often seen the fish create a bow wave past all the other flies on the leader to take the bob-fly, which was creating a wake. The sedge-type flies, incuding the small Muddler Minnow, are the most popular bob flies (apart from the Soldier Palmer and Grenadier). The fly normally used as a bob can be moved down the leader to form the point fly if the wind is strong and the conditions dull.

It often happens that a particular fly on the leader takes more fish than any other. Yet, when the other flies in the tcam are changed, the effectiveness of the former wears off. The object is to formulate a winning team on the leader, so even if one fly on the team is not taking fish, stick with it until the takes cease altogether.

I try to keep the outline of the wet fly to the appropriate size and shape, either winged or wingless, and I prefer sombre flies for most situations. However, the flies being fished together should not all be a similar colour, as this uniform approach will not make the most of their individual effectiveness. For example, if I am using an attractor such as a Dunkeld or Bloody Butcher, I would not usually also include a Wickham's Fancy or Silver Invicta.

The advice I would give to all with regard to wet flies is to keep them simple, keep them small, and make sure that the bob-fly always makes an impression on the water. This impression can be produced by buoyancy on wavey days, and with hackles on days when the water is calmer. The object is to make sure that the trout looks at the flies, not at the leader!

A brown trout caught from the boat.

WET FLIES FOR SINKING-LINE FISHING

Dunkeld
The standard Dunkeld pattern is always worth including on the cast.

Soldier Palmer
Like the Dunkeld, this will attract fish when worked on a fast-sinking line.

Peach Baby Doll
This is a miniature and coloured variation of the highly successful lure designed by Brian Kench. It is simply peach wool wound round a Size 14 long-shank hook to form a fry shape. The tail and shell-back are of the same material and throat hackles are entirely optional. If this fly is going to be successful it will be so quickly, but do not persevere with it if the results are disappointing.

Kingfisher Butcher
This is tied in the same way as the Bloody Butcher, the difference being that the tail is blue kingfisher, the throat hackle hot orange and the body gold tinsel.

Muddler Minnow
Tied in natural colours, this pattern can prove effective but with a sinking line I prefer to tie a black version and a white one. Both have silver bodies and marabou wings of the appropriate colour and an optional fluorescent tag of either red or green. Fished on the point, when retrieved its buoyancy adds life to other flies on the cast, and keeps the cast off the bottom in shallow water.

Mallard and Claret
Tied in the same way as before, it is always worth trying and at times is very effective.

Sweeney Todd
This is really my bastard version of the original pattern by Richard Walker combined with the Viva designed by Bob Church. The body is black floss silk ribbed with silver wire and the thorax is fluorescent green wool. The wing is black squirrel tail. I dispense with a throat hackle. The original Sweeney Todd has a crimson thorax and this also works, but I prefer the green version. Sinking lines should always have a black fly on the cast and this one works well.

Mylar Minnow
This is a pattern that I devised myself, which works exceedingly well on a sinking line. I developed it in order to imitate small fry, to deceive the better fish that rarely fall to 'gimmick' flashy flies. The name is common to all fry imitations that have mylar bodies.

The underbody is made of polystyrene. This gives it some buoyancy and also pads it out for the mylar tubing that is the eventual body material. A tag of fluorescent green is then tied in, and a length of green tinsel long enough to form the back. The Mylar tubing is then slipped over the hook and tied in at the bend and the eye, and the green tinsel is pulled tight over the hook to form a green back. Some olive hackles are added at the throat, and it is possible to add eyes.

I also tie this pattern using gold mylar, a brown tinsel back and orange tail and throat hackles.

Two large rainbows from Ringstead Grange.

Orange Palmer

This pattern lends itself to many variations, and is useful as a bob fly on the cast when there are fish feeding avidly in a confined area. It is simply a short-shank hook covered with gold tinsel, and a hot orange hackle wound along the length of the hook shank in palmer fashion. The body can actually be altered to suite the tastes of the tyer, and a popular variation is orange seal fur ribbed overall with oval gold tinsel. Many different versions are possible, and it is a pattern which should provide pleasure at the fly-tying vice and on the water.

Black Ghost

This first came to my notice as a lure in larger sizes than I currently tie it, and it is effective either way. It combines the black, white and yellow, as well as a silver rib. The visibility of the fly is high whilst it retains its subtlety.

The body is black floss silk ribbed with silver tinsel, the tail and throat hackles are yellow cock fibres. The wing is paired white cock hackles laid back along the hook shank. It is important that the hackles are not too erect, and also that they do not extend beyond the bend of the hook or they will twist around the bend and ruin the life of the fly.

Pheasant-tail Nymphs

When tied with a tail and throat hackles, these patterns appear fry-like in shape. The use of some 'flash', and bright colours in the dressing, make them very effective when worked quickly on a sinking line.

Viva

This fly now needs no introduction to flyfishers in the British Isles. Like the Black Ghost, it started life as a lure, and is most effective when fished in small sizes with other flies on a sinking line.

The body is made from black chenille ribbed with silver tinsel, and the hackle at the throat from black cock fibres. The wing is also black cock hackles, and the attraction of the fly is heightened by a tail of fluorescent green tag.

Again, this is a fly which lends itself to experimentation and many versions come to life in the water. The White Viva is the same pattern in white, and the tail can be changed to any colour one desires, as can the body and wing and throat hackles, to provide many workable variations.

Appetizer

When fishing a sunk line I feel the same way about white lures as I do about black ones; to begin with at least one should be on the cast. The Appetiser was designed by Bob Church and is a superb fry imitation and attractor but is a little fiddly to tie in its smaller form. The body is white chenille ribbed with flat silver tinsel; the tail and throat hackle are mixed green and red cock hackle fibres, and the wing is white marabou with an over-wing of a few squirrel tail fibres. The whole effect is very good and attractive to many trout. I have tied a variation using yellow chenille and yellow marabou which works well in slightly coloured water and on those occasions when you sense that the trout might want something a little different.

These patterns tend to differ from the more usual wet flies since they are for fast-sinking lines, not the slow or neutral density kind. The conditions are usually cooler when fast-sinking line tactics are called upon and the chances are that the fish will not be feeding avidly and need to be coaxed into it. Because of this, most of the patterns resemble small lures or fry imitations.

The use of fluorescent and flashy material can be increased in wet flies that are to be used on a fast-sinking line. If there is less light available, the splash of colour or flash of a fly often helps to attract fish. I have proved this to my own satisfaction many times, although I still keep mainly to fluorescent green, and hardly ever used fluorescent reds and oranges. There are other effects which can be used to assist the action of a fly in the water. I sometimes use a buoyant underbody on a fly in order to make it fish slightly differently from any other fly which the trout might have seen before. The effect I am trying to achieve is a diving darting action. It must be remembered, with this method of fishing, that one is often fishing in front of a drifting boat, and the length of the retrieve is reduced by the forward drift of the boat. As much use as possible must be made of the time that the flies are in the water.

I always use Captain Hamilton heavy-weight hooks for my wet flies, which come in sizes 10 downwards for competition fishing. The largest size I use is size 8, which are only just too big to fit in with international rules.

The use of flash and colour is more tolerable in wet flies fished on a sinking line, because they are often moved more quickly, and are given movement by the sinking of the line and, at the end of the cast, by being lifted through the water and up.

There are also a number of traditional patterns which I recommend for use with those discussed above and which are available from specialist fly-dressing publications. They are Bibio, Ginger Quill, Parmachene Belle, Ivens' Green and Brown Nymph, Invicta, Alexandra and March Brown.

Spooning the contents of a fish's stomach to find out what the fish are feeding on.

DRY FLIES

Bi-Visible
This is a dressing of American origin which is most useful at sedge times. It can be almost any colour one fancies but most often it is brown and white. It is a very simple dry fly to tie, and is two brown cock hackles palmered tightly from the bend to the head and then a white hackle is palmered round the head. The tail consists of cock hackle fibres, or hackle tips for preference. This is a high-floating fly which creates interest, in particular on small waters. A more usual colour is black, which can look like an alder fly or some other black insect at a different time of year to the sedge hatches.

Grey Duster
A tiny fly which is of most use when the caenis are hatching and the trout will take nothing else. It is a relatively simple fly to tie, which is as well because it is more successful in size 14 and smaller! The body is dubbed light grey rabbit's fur and on my preferred patterns the tail fibres and hackle are usually white or pale grey. Occasionally I have taken a lot of trout with this fly.

Crane Fly
This is also known as Daddy-Long-Legs and needs no introduction. The natural is a terrestrial insect which is blown onto the water in large numbers in late summer and early autumn. A long-shank hook is needed and because it is a

large fly I use a light body material such as stripped peacock herl or pheasant tail fibre. There is no tail and the body is wound up to the point where a thorax can be formed. Six legs are tied in at the back of the thorax, the most popular material being pheasant tail fibres, with knots forming the leg joints. Four hackles are tied so that they form the wings and lie flat on the water in spent fashion. Natural cock hackles or badger fibres can be used depending on preference and a cock hackle is then spun round to give the fly the desired buoyancy. The fly should be given a dark or light effect depending on the kind of day, without affecting its attraction to the trout. This fly should always be available when fishing British waters and it will take fish all the year round, though more consistently at the right time of year.

A rainbow trout that fell to a dapped daddy-long-legs.

Black Gnat

This represents almost any dark or black fly which settles on the water. It is comparatively easy to tie, the tail and hackle are black cock hackle fibres, the body is black floss silk and the wings are light starling. This fly is only successful if the sizes are kept to 14 and below.

Gold-Ribbed Hare's Ear

Another traditional, small and very effective pattern, also quite simple to tie. The body is hare's ear ribbed with gold tinsel and the hackle can be the body material picked out or left as it is, although I prefer to do so to provide stability. The tail is three strands of the body material, and the wings are upright starling feathers. This fly can be fished with good results at most times and will take fish during any hatch.

White Moth

For obvious reasons, this pattern is better at dusk. It can be fished as a wake fly, but is very successful at times fished static. The body is traditionally white ostrich herl, but white suede chenille is an ideal substitute. The hackle is several turns of white cock hackle and the wings are white swan or goose. There is, traditionally, a tail of golden pheasant tippets. Having not yet seen any moths with tails I tend to leave them off.

Greenwell's Glory

This pattern is representative of olives or buzzers, and is a very good general dry fly pattern. The wings are tied upright and the hook sizes are small down- or up-eyed from size 12 downwards. The body is pale yellow floss silk ribbed with the finest gold wire. The wing is dark starling, and the hackle either badger or coch-y-bondhu, which is spun behind and forward of the wings. A tail of pale olive cock hackle fibres is optional but essential if olives are present on the water.

Blue Bottle

This is a pattern which does not readily come to mind but is useful to have for those dog days when nothing is happening, not even a hatch. The body is black chenille ribbed with brilliant blue silk and the tail is of the same blue silk in tag form. The wings are pale blue dun hackle points tied flat and sloping back and the head is usually black chenille. There is a black hackle tied in front of the wings.

Dark Sedge

There are many sedge patterns and they are usually successful. The difference lies in the body material and colour. Because of the backward slope of the wings, it is not absolutely necessary to include them, but my own feeling is that they should be included. The most used pattern, generally, is the dark sedge.

The body of the dark sedge, traditionally, is a stripped peacock quill, and a furnace cock hackle is palmered the entire length of the body. Laid over this is a flat wing from a hen pheasant centre tail feather. I usually 'roll' my wings to form a strong outline. The hackle is then again a furnace cock hackle spun in front of the wings.

The numerous sedge patterns work mainly because they adhere to the same basic shape of the natural fly. The sedge is a prolific and popular fly and I don't know where we would be without it during the summer months and calm evenings. The imitation is also successful when skated over the surface.

Dry flies on stillwater are something of an anomaly. They are more common on small stillwaters than on the large windswept reservoirs, lakes and lochs. If the conditions are right, however, they can be deadly on any water, particularly during the evening rise.

I recall that during 1987, regulars at Grafham Water were reputed to be carrying out regular execution from the boats with dry fly, and this was fairly early in the season. At the time it was a closely guarded secret because of the team events which were going on in a number of competitions. Those of us who knew the water well, but not perhaps quite as well as the locals, were prepared to believe what we heard but were sceptical. It seemed an unlikely method for that time of year and throughout the day, and we also considered it might be a 'red herring'. Our disbelief and scepticism were soon dispelled when one of the members of the team fished with a local angler in the boat. What he effectively did was to cast the fly out in front of the boat and retrieve just enough line to keep in touch with the fly – and no more. With the fly dead on the water the trout readily, and often, rose to it.

This goes to show that it is always as well to be prepared, either from boat or bank, and to be versatile in your approach.

From the bank, it is often the case that a dry fly

may be at a considerable distance from the angler when compared with fishing the dry fly on streams or rivers. It is also easier to pin-point the fly on running water from the direction of the line; on stillwaters we have the problem of perspective – we know in which direction the fly lies but we are not so sure how far away it is unless it is in constant sight and being concentrated upon. For these reasons, larger-than-necessary dry flies are often used on stillwaters at inappropriate times. As an example there is the Bi-visible Sedge being fished during a buzzer hatch. This makes the fly visible to the angler but it is out of character with what is happening round the trout, so a fish will often cease to rise after it has approached a

fly on the surface that does not look 'right' or natural.

Again, there are many patterns which ought to have been included above, such as the Lake Olive, Ginger Quill, a variety of Duns and Mayflies and so on, all of which can be found in the fly-tying books which abound, and in my own fly box. All those mentioned here will take trout on nearly every occasion. Stillwater trout tend to be less choosey than stream fish, except in a prolific hatch, and on days when the fish are rising relatively freely they will come to one of these patterns.

Contemplating a change.

LURES FOR STILLWATER FISHING

Platinum Blonde

A lure which I know will fool specimen trout. It is a simple tying on a large long-shank lure hook. A length of white bucktail is tied in at the bend and the body is formed by winding silver tinsel or lurex to the eye, where another length of white bucktail is tied in to form a wing. The fly is a streamer in every sense of the word and I gleaned the pattern from an American book written by the late Joe Brooks, who also recommended the Honey Blonde, which is yellow bucktail with a gold body, tied the same. I have caught a good many above-average trout with it. The Platinum Blonde is always best fished deep and slow at any time of the year. I consider bucktail and any other soft hair to be the best material for wings and I do dislike the cut-off ends which to me make a square and unnatural look and, I suspect, to the trout.

Tandem Appetiser

A pattern which is exactly the same as the one described in the wet fly section and it is included here for the purpose of introducing tandem lures. On days when there has been a prolific hatch I have taken fish on a tandem as it sank through the water on its way to trout lying deep. The trick with the tandem is to make the link stiff enough not to kink round the fly at the front when it is being cast and to keep the wings the right length for the same reason. I prefer a link made of knotted monofilament which has been straightened and then whipped and glued to both hooks.

The fly is then tested to make sure that it will not slip before the dressing is completed. Monofilament is best because if it is strong enough it has stiffness and flexibility for when it is being retrieved.

Black-and-Silver Lure

A simple fly which I would not be without in the early season. The tail and throat hackles are black cock hackles as is the wing formed by two pairs back-to-back, and the body is silver tinsel, mylar or lurex. The sizes I prefer are 8 or 10 long-shank because I have had trout on these sizes, whereas I have rarely had much success when using larger hooks. This lure is most effective when it is fished slowly.

Missionary

This is another fly that I would not want to be without. The late Dick Shrive showed me how to tie this and it has caught trout for me ever since. Early one morning on Farmoor Reservoir I played a brown trout for 20 minutes on this fly before the fish managed to free itself. This trout was well into double figures and in clear water was under the rod-tip for most of the time. The body of this fly is white chenille ribbed with tinsel and the throat hackle and tail fibres are white cock (even though the original tying had red). The wing is a teal feather tied flat over the body of the fly so that it flutters in the water. The head is finished with red varnish. As a fry imitator, this fly succeeds very well all the year round and really comes into its own in the situation where the angler is fishing near weedbeds and the light is fading.

Muddler Minnows

I frequently use these, tied in the same fashion as the wet fly style except that I substitute hair wings for the marabou. These can be successful as wake flies or fished near the bank on a slow-sinking line.

Diving Muddler

A fly which I devised to catch trout feeding on fry. The body, on a long-shank hook, is mylar tied over a base of polystyrene to give size and a buoyant base. A tail is optional, mine are usually orange wool; the wing is white marabou with an overlay of hair of any colour one fancies, but I use white or natural squirrel tail. The head is white deer hair spun and clipped Muddler-fashion. The complete tying was planned to attract a trout in every way: it had the flash of a turning fish, the white head gave visibility in fading light, and the orange tag triggered aggression, and at the same time the head created a wake. I always fish this on a sinking line, casting it near weedbeds or to rising fish and then leaving it. The fly floats while the line sinks and when the retrieve is made the fly ploughs across the surface, then dives as it follows the line. Takes are usually vicious and can come at any time during the retrieve.

Goldie

Another Bob Church invention, similar to the Honey Blonde in construction except that the tail and throat are yellow cock hackle fibres. The body is gold lurex or tinsel and the wing yellow bucktail overlaid with a few fibres of black squirrel tail. Tied as a tandem, this fly has proved a killer of big brown trout and is very good in late season, or any time of the year when fished deep.

Floating Fry

A lure which is fished as a dry fly! It has become very popular on British reservoirs and has accounted for many large trout. Basically, it is just a hook-shank spun its whole length with white deer hair which is then clipped to the shape of a tiny perch. The effect is better if the final trimming is done with a very sharp blade. The fly is then coloured to represent the perch and is fished near weedbeds and any area where trout are known to be feeding on fry. It will be taken while static or if it is being twitched. The hook-bend should be down when the fly is resting on the water. Tying it takes a lot of patience and effort to produce the perfect fly but in this case it is worth it. It is really a late summer and autumn fly.

Orange Lure

A large version of the Whisky Fly and one which really can be whatever you want it to be and no box should be without a range of these lures. I always use gold bodies for mine and prefer calf's tail for the bulk that it provides. For me, tail and throat hackles are optional because this lure is fished very quickly in an attempt to provoke the trout into taking.

Viva

This has caught fish for me in larger sizes than those for wet fly. The body is black chenille ribbed with silver and the tail is fluorescent green. Throat hackle and wings are black cock hackles tied in the same way as the previous pattern. It can be fished faster due to the green tail which will attract and arouse 'aggression' more than the plain version. The Black Chenille is the same as this fly but with black cock hackles for the tail instead of the green tag, but it also works well with a red tag.

Kate Russell

I designed this lure intending to provide flash and attraction. This one has a silver body with a fluorescent green tag for the tail and a hot orange calf's tail wing. It works better in the smaller sizes and as a dropper when in conjunction with a larger drab fly on the point. It worked well right from the beginning and has continued so to do at all times of the year. I wish I could say that about all of my fly creations!

Wag-Tail Lures

A range of flies which was introduced by Fred Wagstaffe, an innovative and competent angler from the Midlands. It began when I bought a couple of sand-eel imitations while replacing some fly-tying material. I never used the sand-eels and gave them to Bev Perkins who in turn passed them to Wagstaffe, who then introduced them as 'Waggies'. They have now been used so extensively that most large trout are 'educated' about them and their unique tail-wagging movements, which are supplemented by whatever dressing one takes a fancy to, and Appetiser and Goldie are very popular. These flies can be difficult to cast because of their weight and are usually fished from a drifting boat for the constant motion it provides to keep the tail wagging. It is fair to say that their use is frowned upon.

Leaded Lures

Rather like a jig-fly, these started out a few years ago as flies which were weighted at the head, providing a diving action when being retrieved. The movement was accentuated by the use of a flowing marabou tail tied in at the bend of the hook. I prefer to lightly lead these lures all the way along the hook-shank, and I use mylar for the body to give the fly sparkle. The tail is of marabou, any colour, for it is the movement which attracts the trout. Sometimes I palmer a hackle of red or orange along the length of the body to add more effect. These lures are open to experimentation and are effective everywhere. I use a medium-length hook-shank of Size 8 or 10. They catch fish all year fished fast or slowly.

This is one area where every budding and experienced fly-tyer can experiment to his heart's content. Lures also fall into the categories of imitators or attractors and I maintain that the silhouette of the fly is just as important on a lure as it is on a nymph, although in more recent years it has been proved just how important to the fish are the movement of the fly and the colour. Size is important in that an average trout will not usually attempt to take a very large lure, although one of this kind is the sort that will take a specimen fish from deep water, as long as the lure is sufficiently well disguised.

PART TWO

TROUT FISHING ON RIVERS

TROUT FISHING ON RIVERS

In all the time that I have spent trout fishing I have learned most about fish behaviour from observation and dedicated fishing in the clear waters of chalkstreams. If one can see the fish it may be possible to understand the reasons for any particular reaction and at the same time one can become better and better in the art of presenting the fly correctly. Chalkstream flyfishing is an education that no flyfisherman should miss, especially if there is the remotest chance of following the sport on a water that allows observation of the trout once a fly has been presented to it.

Although the most famous of them are found in the South of England, trout waters of this kind are not peculiar to that area, they can be found in every part of the British Isles. Some of the moorland streams in Scotland and the West Country may not be as clear as the Hampshire chalkstreams but they still allow the trout to be seen and therefore contribute equally to the flyfisherman's education – and do not cost as much to fish.

The plump trout in the food-rich southern English rivers are not that size in moorland streams and even wilder waters but given the chance on the right tackle they do provide superb sport. I have found this to be so as much on the streams of Dartmoor, the rivers of Derbyshire and Yorkshire, the large and small rivers of Scotland as I have fishing the classic chalksteams.

All such waters provide excellent sport and their size is for ever secondary to the euphoria one experiences in these delightful surroundings. While fishing a chalkstream, with its neatly clipped and trimmed banks, I have loved the challenge of stalking some obstinate trout in an overlooked part of the water, warily feeding beneath some low and overhanging branches.

These waters have in common deep stretches, holes, fast runs, weedbeds and other features which provide more attractive and challenging places to seek a trout than almost any stillwater.

It is true that in the British Isles the wild trout do not reach the size they grow to on the large continents. Of course, there are now generous fishery owners who attempt to compensate by growing trout to a substantial size and then releasing them in their waters.

It is a test of fishing skill to land a large stock-bred trout in running water but the fish will not have the strength that it would have acquired had it always been in the river searching and struggling for natural food.

RIVER SPECIES
Apart from a few isolated cases, the only trout in British rivers are the brown and the rainbow trout, which, again, is being introduced and the Derbyshire Wye does have a breeding colony, some of which I have been fortunate enough to catch. They are small but perfect specimens and are a delight to bring to the net. There are unsubstantiated claims of the species breeding in other rivers but I have no certain information about this.

STEELHEAD Above right *This is a native of North America and has been successfully introduced into Britain. In some rivers into which it has been introduced (or into which it has escaped), it has run to sea. Some have subsequently been recorded returning to the river again. A particularly strong fighter, it grows to weights in excess of 20 lb (9 kg) and responds well to downstream fishing techniques using wet flies or bright lures. It will also take dry flies.*

BROWN TROUT Right *This is a stream brown trout and they do vary in coloration from water to water. There are two basic varieties which have been distributed throughout the world: the Austrian/German brown and the British brown. In most instances it is not possible to distinguish between them, although originally the former was more colourful. The British version was distributed to North America, Australia, New Zealand, India and other countries in the nineteenth century and came from Loch Leven, in Scotland.*

Given the right conditions, brown trout breed readily and are widespread. Some isolated streams and rivers holding this fish are neglected, perhaps because of their location and nature and a limited demand for this kind of fishing. But when they are found they are a delight and joy to fish and will provide sport with small, wild and very fast trout.

TACKLE REQUIRED

In all small waters one's tackle depends very much on personal preference and is dictated by the water itself. Generally, for the average stream or small river, I use a rod no longer than 7ft 6in (2.3m) and in fact favour the short rod I have mentioned earlier, the 6ft (1.8m) 'Midge'. If the water is fairly broad one must have a rod long enough to allow proper control over the fly. However, if the rod has to have sufficient through-action to allow fly presentation properly, trying to achieve length at the same time will make it ungainly and awkward to use.

To get distance, it is possible to use a longer rod with more tip action and this is acceptable if that distance is maintained. But there is the danger of poor presentation if you try to shorten the range with the same rod, and I have found that a fair distance can be obtained with a shorter rod with the use of a weight-forward line of a light AFTM rating.

In all my river fishing I prefer the Cortland Nymph-tip for its handling qualities and visibility. It is weight-forward, light and has advantages where there is a restricted back cast or the cast has to be kept low. These situations do not allow the luxury of a double-taper line even though it has a slower, more pleasing action, with an elegant turn-over of the fly on delivery.

Personal preference also dictates the choice of rod material, and I have never set foot on a riverbank in pursuit of trout with anything other than split-cane or greenheart unless circumstances have forced me to act otherwise. This can be summed up by my penchant for using natural materials when surrounded by nature – but I confess that when salmon fishing I do not use horse-hair lines or a 16ft (4.8m) cane rod!

There is something special and different in the feel of cane, particularly when playing a trout, and the action when casting gives much more pleasure than when using anything other than boron. The slower action of cane is an advantage in helping one to give a neater delivery of the fly when it matters.

I usually use level lengths of monofilament for leaders, but I acknowledge that better presentation can be obtained with tapered casts. The effect of this can be achieved by knotting lengths of different strengths of monofilament together, terminating with the finer diameter piece nearest the fly. But I have now stopped doing this because for me it did not improve presentation to any appreciable degree. For me, the problems with tapered casts are purely psychological in that I prefer to be free to choose my preferred brand of monofilament, and the commerically produced tapered casts do not supply them.

If I used one of them and a trout was put down I would instantly blame the tapered cast and revert to my own approach which has stood me in good stead. I also prefer to maintain a fine presentation of the tackle where and when necessary and here the heavier butt of the tapered cast seems to me to be alien. If the final delivery is crisp and powerful enough the fly will turn over nicely and the correct presentation has been achieved.

At one time disregarding it, I now consider the reel to be of paramount importance and having used many different kinds and models I have come to prefer the lightweight kinds manufactured in graphite. These reels are much lighter than the metal kinds and they give a faster reaction when the angler is striking and playing a fish. This is of course not always desirable or necessary but sometimes an extra split-second can make all the difference. There are some very nice reels in the top quality range, but while they are aesthetically pleasing I do not reach for them when I am in the tackle shop.

IDENTIFICATION OF LIES

All rivers have small fisheries within larger ones and there are very few stretches of a water that do not hold trout if the river is well stocked, although I have fished waters where the trout have been unaccountably absent.

Different types of stream provide different types of lies.
Top right *In a chalkstream, lies are provided by weeds and gravel, with bank features also being important.*
Right *A freestone stream provides many interesting features and lies for the trout, such as large stones and overhanging shrubs.*

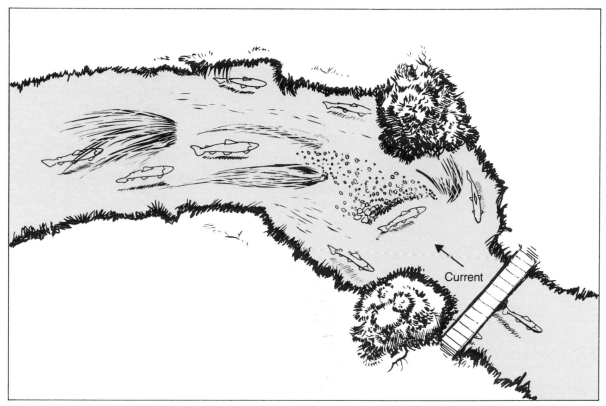

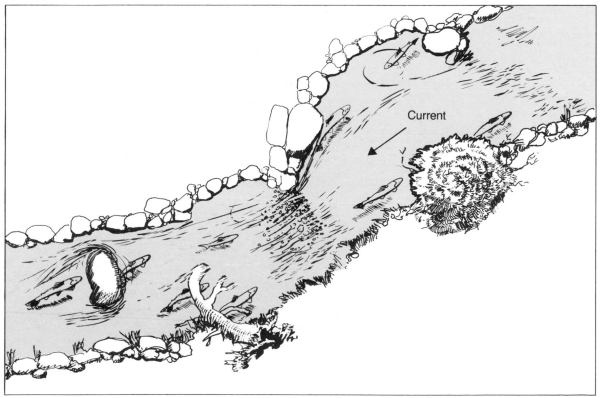

Left *An angler fishing downstream wet fly on the River Wharfe, Yorkshire.*

Above *The ultimate for every dry-fly fisherman: a 'Wild West' spring creek in Montana, USA, where double-figure brown trout rise to the fly in clear water. These superb surroundings provide some of the best sport available anywhere in the world.*

If there is a deep hole it will always hold trout and they will always be present in deep water that has a fast current running through it, and these fish are always difficult to approach. Trout also have other favourite lies against the far banks where there are bends with an uneven depth. There may be a hatch or some feature with a sharp drop over which water tumbles and where the bottom has been scoured to form a hole and here one will always find fish.

Remember, an important point about all features of this kind is that the current at the surface is always considerably faster than it is at the bottom. It creates a kind of oxygen-rich 'lounge' where the trout can lie and laze, picking off food particles that come their way without having to fight against a current in order to reach them.

In rivers, trout tend to become territorial and will not move far from their lies unless forced to do so. They occupy a stretch of water where their food comes to them on the current and remain there throughout the day. If the area is reasonably shallow they leave if the sun warms the water too much, but when it becomes shaded they will return. Trees and bushes which hang over or close to the water provide this kind of area and the chances of finding trout there are always good.

APPROACHING THE TROUT

If a trout is aware of the presence of an angler it will either be more cautious or leave the area immediately. In the former case the fish will become agitated and will move away if disturbed or cast to repeatedly, so rest the fish and try later. If there is plenty of fishable water available I mark the fish and leave quietly, to return very cautiously later for another try. That fish will have returned to its usual position to feed if it has been given enough time.

In deeper water one can cast to a trout time and time again without alarming it, and I recall a rainbow of over 4lb (1.8kg) (which had grown on and put on weight) which I had cast to for a quarter of an hour. It involved changing the fly pattern several times until I found the one which tempted it and had a feeling of exaltation when at last it took instead of just following or showing mild interest. The occasion was notable because I had to cast from between two large trees and was practically on top of that trout!

The pool was a small hole at the end of a turbulent stretch of water, the bank was overhung with vegetation and I can still see the dark shadow of that fish on the dappled bottom, then rising in the water with its white mouth opening and closing on the nymph, then turning back before the rod arched and the bucking of the trout came through to my wrist. Due to my restricted stance I had a few anxious moments as I played it.

With me, approaching trout in clear water is something of an anomaly and I have never agreed with the standard views about trout vision because my experiences tell me otherwise. A fish has often bolted away downstream as I approached it even when I should not have been in its sight and my footfall was not heavy enough to alarm it. At other times I have approached a fish to a point where I have been level with it, have cast to it and caught it. A trout in that position should have had me well within its range of vision and it ought to have been off before I could get a fly onto the water.

There is no doubt that refraction contributes to trout vision, or perhaps lack of it. The lower the profile the angler presents the easier it is to approach a trout and I always carry the rod butt-forward at these times. It is not then several feet in front of the angler and moving, so any 'educated' trout will react accordingly, particularly if the rod has very flashy whippings or a reflective finish.

As I have just said, I have caught trout while virtually standing over them, but the water meadows that I fish on the River Kennet, in Berkshire, have as one feature a stretch of varying depths with steep banks. Now, however stealthily I approach the trout there, and there are some very good specimens, they always seem to be aware of an angler much earlier than the fish in the main river and bolt for a deep lie. If a fly is presented to them there they dash away again. I have never been able to reason their behaviour out. It has made fishing that stretch a great challenge but I have been able to take a number of trout there. They are always good fish and put up a stout fight.

So far as the trout are concerned the visibility of the angler is determined by his height above the surface, the nature of that surface and the depth of the fish. A turbulent surface makes the approach much easier than a smooth one. Clothing might have an effect and I feel that for a sensible and successful approach to a water one should use common sense, be able to know how far one can go, keep a low profile, move slowly and wear sombre clothing. Once you are too near you have lost the opportunity to make a successful cast to the trout.

TROUT FOOD IN RIVERS AND STREAMS

All rivers and streams have many items of food in common and lack of food in rocky waters and moorland streams means that the fish will take any fly or lure that is cast to them in the correct way. But this lack of natural food can also mean that their instinct for survival is stronger, so hunger does not always lead to their downfall and they still demand a degree of skill and sharp reflexes from the angler.

The food present in these waters includes nymphs, which hatch as flies, and sub-surface insect life such as corixae or other waterbeetles. There are also small fish but my casual observation has never spotted the presence of minnows.

In early season there is the small black hawthorn fly, and their hatch often induces a trout rise; then as the season progresses the olives feature strongly but the most glorious of all is the mayfly. Those are the flies most often seen near rivers and streams, with others such as the March Brown. Bankside observation is the only way to determine which fly is over or on the water and attracting feeding trout.

ETIQUETTE

The way one approaches another angler when river fishing is more critical than in stillwater fly-fishing and it also differs with the kind of water being fished.

On chalkstreams and the better-stocked waters it is likely that the angler will be allotted a beat and perhaps a ghillie. This makes things simple and prevents any intrusion into your fishing area and stops you straying into another's.

But on the far more commonplace club and association waters you are sure to come into contact with fellow anglers and if everyone has due regard and respect for all then amiable and pleasant sport can be equally enjoyed.

If an angler has taken up station and is casting to a fish he must be given absolute precedence and no approach to him should be made without invitation, and this includes passing him to fish ahead. If it is possible to fish ahead he must be given as wide a berth as possible so that any trout that could be covered by the first angler is not put down or alerted. It is better to wait until the angler is aware of your presence and then ask if it is all right to go on.

In downstream fishing, if there is an angler ahead it is as well to fish as close to him as you think fit, matching his speed with yours, but bearing in mind that he will already have covered the water. The best thing to do is to give one another plenty of space. Leaving your stretch and moving ahead of another angler is unforgivable. This may sound elementary but there are anglers who walk past and move into a pool that you have been patiently and hopefully working your way towards with a lot of care and anticipation. It has happened on many occasions to me and to my friends and can be avoided very easily with forethought and consideration.

There is a golden rule in trout fishing when one finds oneself in close proximity of another angler: take stock of the situation and wait, and then ask yourself, 'If I were that angler what would I be doing next and how would I like him to treat my position if the roles were reversed?'

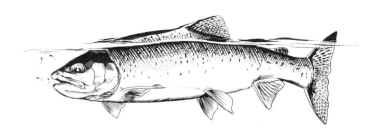

Left *With the Rocky Mountain foothills providing a backdrop, Jack Hemmingway (eldest son of Ernest Hemmingway) fishes a spring creek in Montana, USA.*
Above *Many of the spring-fed streams in the American West are easily wadable, and are not unlike the chalk streams of England. However, in these surroundings the peace and quiet, solitude, and proximity to nature that fishing provides, take on a new meaning.*

DRY-FLY FISHING

When fishing the dry fly it is important to be prepared with a number of patterns and these will be discussed later in this chapter. Much of the mystique surrounding streams and rivers is misguided and born of long-dead chivalrous egos rather than the nature of the trout. However, do not take this to imply that I decry certain attitudes towards dry-fly fishing, for I wholeheartedly support the gentle-mannered approach. What I mean is that this facet of fishing, so long as it is carried out in the correct manner, is not nearly so difficult or as complicated as anglers have been led to believe.

The colour of the fly is always important when matching the hatch, then size is the next decision to be made. In my opinion the artificial does not have to be a precise imitation of the natural insect, but what is important is how and where it is presented in relation to the depth of water. This includes the 'height' at which the fly floats. If the trout are taking dry fly they might ignore one riding high on top of the surface film but greedily take one in it, and the reverse also applies.

A high-floating fly will have more chance of being taken on a bright day because of its visibility, but if it does not dent the surface film it can be less effective on a dull day. In contrast, a fly floating in the surface film on a sunless day is much more visible to the trout because a halo of light surrounds the artificial and outlines it.

So I contend that size, outline and presentation are more important than colour and closeness of imitation. The most successful Mayfly pattern I tie is one that hardly floats and which has to be treated to sit in the surface film, but on numerous waters it works far better than any other Mayfly pattern.

There are many days when the trout do not rise steadily even though they can be seen in one area. If the dry fly is favoured, or it is the only method allowed on the water, a trout can be induced to rise by a fly being constantly cast over it. The approach must be tailored to suit the position of the fish, the current and the angle of the cast.

Because of the control it gives the angler, the best way to cast the dry fly to a trout is from a downstream position. In fact, in some quarters it is considered against the rules and bad etiquette to fish in any other way. Having decided on the fly pattern, take a minute or so to watch the trout's behaviour and the flow of water. There are very few occasions when specimen-sized trout will lie in a position which allows them to be easily covered, for there is usually some disturbance to the current which requires the angler to think about avoiding the drag which will occur. These situations demand the exercise of caution and expertise.

The variations of current mean that presentation from downstream is easier, because casting straight across a varied current produces drag on the fly which will alert the trout. The object of casting upstream to the fish is that it gives the trout just sufficient time to 'recognize' it as food and rise to it. If the fly behaves unnaturally, dragging behind or across the current, the trout will not respond to it as food.

There are a few exceptions when trout will rise instantly to seize a fly which has begun to drag, but it is not a method to try on one's first approach and cast: it is a style to use when all else has failed. The major problem with a dragging fly,

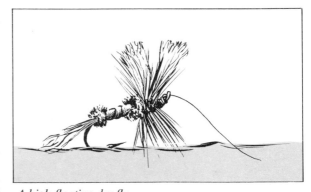

A high-floating dry fly.

apart from its unnatural action, is that it makes the leader visible to the fish. One way to avoid drag affecting the fly is to cast more line than is required so that the drag affects the fly line but not the leader. It might be possible to keep the rod held up, so lifting the line from the water, but in my experience it has never been that simple and commonsense has been needed to solve the problem.

When casting the dry fly, the depth of the trout must be taken into account. There will have to be an 'over-cast' so that the fly settles beyond and upstream of where the fish lies. Accuracy is essential, because while trout will sometimes move a short distance to take a fly they will not usually go far.

The fly must not pass the trout at a distance which allows it to examine the artificial, for it may not be acceptable for some reason. It is far better to let the fly travel over the fish from directly upstream. If the presentation is poor, allow the fly to get well behind the trout before lifting it off for another attempt. Do not lift it from water up-stream of the fish where it can be seen, for it will disturb the fish and probably allow it to see the tackle.

Try to let the fly settle on the water at exactly the right spot so that any drag will occur after it has passed over the fish, or – hopefully – after it has been taken! But it is not easy and the correct presentation is made more difficult if there is a cross-wind or one blowing downstream. In any form of river and stream fishing the most favour-able wind is an upstream breeze; it assists delivery of the fly and ruffles the water surface to obscure the trout's vision.

The 'over-cast' used to eliminate drag is achieved by making a high delivery of the fly and keeping the rod-tip well up as the fly touches the water and in that split-second dropping the rod to give enough slack line on the water to allow the fly to drift over the fish. Ideally, one should have some slack in the leader which will be unravelled by the drag, to leave the fly drifting naturally on the current.

There are other ways of combating drag which require that one mends the line by the use of the rod. It is effective but must be avoided if it is going to cause any disturbance on the surface which will be visible to the trout – the trouble is, you really cannot tell if this is so until you try it! If the current between you and the fish is fast and the trout is lying in slack water you can avoid disturbance by staying as far downstream as possible and casting to the fish, mending the line upstream if possible.

The problem is worse when the trout is lying in fast water on the far side of a slack area. What happens is that the fly is whisked downstream on the current while the slack water holds the line stationary, immediately exerting drag, and it is difficult to cure because the fish usually lies in the current against the slack water. Again, a cast from well downstream is preferable to one across the current, but mending the line on slack water produces much more disturbance than if it were being carried downstream.

It is not usually necessary to carry the fly very far over the trout before it takes or not, and so long as the presentation is made at the point where the fly enters the trout's vision, and con-tinues on the current towards the fish, you should catch it. A trout will often turn and take a fly as it goes downstream, so watch the fish as well as the fly, for its intentions are often patently obvious by its movements. You can tell when it is interested

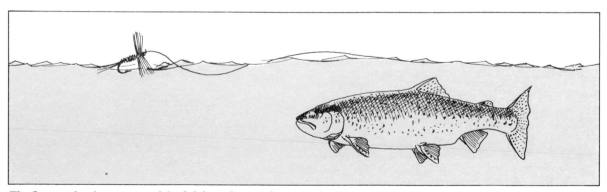

The fly must land upstream of the fish by at least as far as the depth of the fish in the water.

Left *Stalking rising fish on an English chalkstream. The banks on chalkstreams are often soft and cleared of vegetation, the current is slow and the water clear. The fisherman must move stealthily in order not to frighten the fish away.*
Top *In completely contrasting surroundings, this*

fisherman looks for trout on an Australian Western Lakes feeder stream.
Above *A river-keeper at work on the River Test, Hampshire, England, cutting weed growth. This clearing of the weeds on chalkstreams means that the fish can be visible to the angler – and vice versa.*

Mending the line to counteract 'drag'. When the line reaches point (x), mend it in an upstream direction.

in the fly because its fins begin to move rapidly, but of course this does not indicate that it is about to take. At the same time, 'fanning' of the fins also leads to a sudden panic-stricken flight.

The trout may rise slowly in the water, showing that it is about to inspect the fly, but if the current is swift the fish will not take it. The same action in fast water tells you that the fish is genuinely interested. In slow water, a steadily rising fish usually means that it is likely to take the offering. If it does not, having inspected the fly it will drop down again and during the next cast the trout will either rise and take or ignore the fly. Any agitation shown by the fish will tell you to change the fly or rest the fish and move.

If the fly is ignored the trout is unaware of it and you could try changing the fly and make the cast more accurate, but I prefer to fish on with the same artificial until I am sure that it is the pattern or the size of the fly which is not invoking any interest. At the same time as you change the fly, reduce its size too. But just change the size of the fly if the fish has shown any interest at all. It is surprising what immediate effect a smaller fly can have, turning an apparently disinterested trout into a hungry one.

For reasons of presentation I usually use a spun hackle on a fly because the up-winged versions can have serious problems as well as not always being appropriate. Instead of floating, they may lie flat on their side with one of the wings flat on the surface instead of with the wings upright; in other words they are not imitating one of those beautiful ephemerids twirling away on the current and the trout will ignore them.

If the fly does not allow correct presentation, the problem lies in its tying, so avoid the temptation to tie up-winged flies with wings so long that they overbalance when they are on the surface. A well-hackled fly is effective because its body construction makes all the difference. I also prefer a rougher outline on dry flies and get this with seal's fur, rabbit or hare's ear.

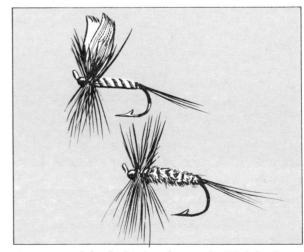

An upwinged dry fly (top) and a spun hackled dry fly.

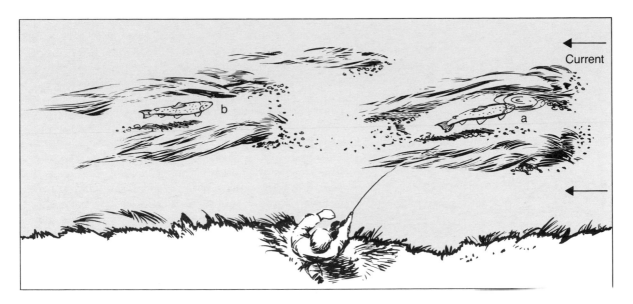

Current

This angler would stand more chance of landing fish (b) than fish (a).

If you are trying for near-exact imitation a lifelike segmented effect can be achieved with a quill body. If it is good enough it will be taken by trout, for nothing short of perfection will be acceptable.The use of tinsel in the dressing for ribbing will eliminate some of the buoyancy, but a high-floating fly is good so far as the angler's visibility is concerned and I would rather see my flies floating in the surface film or only slightly higher.

On many occasions I have seen anglers dry-fly fishing and making numerous false casts in the immediate vicinity of the trout, which may do nothing but show the fly line to the fish, probably sending it away before the cast is made, and any fish scared off will transmit its fright to others. So do not first approach a fish and then strip line off the reel while false-casting. The correct action is to settle into the casting position, pull sufficient line off the reel to reach the fish and cast to it, any false-casting should be done out of the trout's field of vision.

Once the fish has been covered you then have the correct length of line out to enable you to cast to the fish again and again without needing to make false casts. The ideal is to pick the line up, make one false cast behind, then cover the trout, but the retrieve after covering the fish sometimes makes this impossible.

If the trout is upstream and the fly correctly drifting down towards it, you have to retrieve line at a rate fast enough to keep up with the current, and in this way the fly will not be moved on the surface. When the fish rises and takes the fly it is essential that it is given enought time to turn back down with it before the strike is made. If its head is still tilted upwards a strike will snatch the fly away from it. This rarely does any harm, but is not desirable. However, if in doing so you prick the trout it will certainly dash away and you will have to seek another fish elsewhere.

Sometimes I have missed a fish more than once while striking before finally hooking and netting it. The length of time between the fly being taken and the strike will as always depend upon how fast the trout has approached the fly. A slashing rise can lead to an almost instantaneous strike and on the other hand a leisurely take is a test of nerve, leaving the angler wondering if the trout is going to eject the artificial before he decides to strike, which should be just firm enough to set the hook. The pressure must then be kept on until you know how the fish will react to the hook.

In running water, the trout has advantages that the stillwater kind do not enjoy, including the streamerweed that trout seem to be able to put to such good use. Almost without fail they can spot a problem area before the angler does and a fish can be lost very easily unless speed and ability are employed.

Always have the trout upstream of the rod; in this way the fish not only has to fight the spring in

Left *Fishing a spate river that has its 'bones' showing. The wild brown trout found in this type of river are not necessarily large, but their constant battle against the current makes them very strong, and they provide excellent sport when hooked.*
Top *Special care is needed when wading in these conditions because the river-bed will be very uneven and the rocks slippery.*
Above *A perfect brown trout, taken on a dry fly, lies beaten on the surface, ready for the net or release.*

the rod but since it is trying to turn its head and swim back upstream it has the current to contend with as well. The other advantage is that if it reaches a weedbed it can be coaxed out with comparative ease, which is not the case when it is in weed from the downstream position.

As always, sidestrain can play an important part of playing a trout in a current. Those bold dashes made by trout in fast water holding scattered obstacles can be heart-stopping and their memory will warm the winter evenings for years to come when anglers are browsing over past fishing trips.

One of my most memorable trout weighed 2½lb (1.3kg) and was caught on a dry fly I was fishing in a small chalkstream. The fish had been lying under some bushes which in places touched the water. One bush was only three or four yards (2.7–3.6m) downstream of a bridge with three arches and the lie was on the opposite bank.

The cast had to be accurate because I knew that the trout which occupied that lie were usually sizeable by the standards of the water and the first cast took the fly almost to those trailing branches, then the fly was taken. I had to do something before the line was carried into the branches and the line tightened as I struck and lifted clear of the water and the fish was on.

I put as much pressure as I dared on the trout because I had to get it from among those bushes, but into the open water it came. Then the fish bolted upstream towards the bridge, from which brambles were trailing into the water as well as debris of all kinds clinging to it. The fish was determined and seemed unstoppable on my light leader and rod, but then it turned and rushed downstream, round the bushes and back up and under them.

At this point I thought I had lost this trout, to be left with nothing but the pleasure of having deceived it into taking a fly from an exceedingly difficult lair. To have kept the rod up would have meant the line going through the branches and I could not follow it because, as usual, I was stuck between two trees. So I let the line go slack and lowered the rod tip and to my surprise the trout came out again and was off swimming down-stream of me as fast as it could.

I applied sidestrain on the fish, turned it and gingerly recovering line against the fast current brought it upstream where it again shot across the current and back under the bushes! Here, for sure, was the parting of the ways, but that trout responded to my slack line as it had done before and was still full of fight. There was more dashing about and yet another excursion into those bushes before the skirmish was brought to a close as I got it into slack water, finally netting a superbly muscled, well-mended cock rainbow.

It is the capture of fish such as that which makes up for many of the disadvantages of life in general and provides wonderful recollections for those dull days when we cannot go fishing.

Where trees and bushes abound along a river or stream they invariably attract fish and although the trout there may not be many they are usually quality fish. It is well to try these places with caution and make every effort to be as sharp with the reactions as most certainly the trout will be.

The fish usually lie at the upstream end of trailing branches and so long as the fly is pre-sented accurately, properly and without disturb-ance you stand a good chance of catching one, because this kind of lie is often avoided by other anglers. Sometimes the evidence of previous failed attempts festoons the branches – and some of them are mine!

Casting Under Obstacles

A strong and low final delivery of the cast is the answer if the space where the fly has to land is restricted by branches. The normally casual, attractive style which produces a wide loop on the back cast, with an easy delivery of the kind made on open water, will not do in constricted places.

The power must be applied for longer so that the rod is well down after the fly has gone forward. This produces a tighter loop and makes the fly turn over with more force than normal, so projecting it into the required area. Timing has to be very accurate here so that the line does not hit the water with a splash. This is not an easy casting method and anything near to perfection can only be achieved with constant, regular practice.

Where branches overhang but do not touch the water and you want to cast under them, the sideways cast is useful. In this way the rod is kept almost parallel to the surface so that false casts and final delivery will be horizontal. It needs an obstruction-free area behind and, again, there has to be more power applied to keep the loop tight. Disturbance to the water is much more likely with this style of casting but if the required presenta-tion can be achieved it is gratifying to see a trout rise to your fly which has needed a good deal of deliberation and patience in its presentation.

I have always believed that trout which lie in difficult places 'feel safe' and will more readily rise to a fly that is presented to them than fish which remain in open water. This is probably because they do not get as much attention from anglers but on the other hand they usually appear to be old enough to have developed strong survival instincts.

Food for Thought

There is no hard-and-fast rule for fishing the dry fly and it is sometimes brought home in the most frustrating circumstances. Ideally, the best time to learn more about trout is when they are taking freely and rising regularly. The mayfly hatch is such a time and there have been occasions when I was taught a lesson by the fish because I was being too casual.

The first instance concerns the River Kennet, where a very plump trout was rising to a prolific hatch but which ignored every Mayfly of varying sizes that I put over it. I was convinced that the fish would eventually take a fly because it was unconcerned by my presence. A dozen or so casts

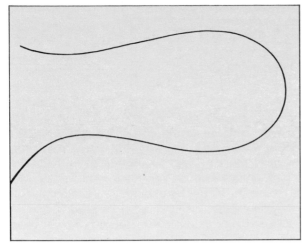
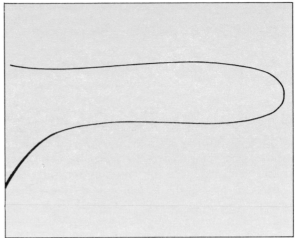

Left The loop made by a normal cast.
Right If the loop is kept tight, it will be much easier to cast under obstacles or into the wind.

proved me wrong and I began to think and, more importantly, watch that trout.

I saw that it did not take every natural mayfly that drifted over it, but selected those that were still living, twitching on the surface. This was confirmed as I watched, there was definitely a preference for the living insects, all the spent ones were ignored and left to drift downstream. I cast again upstream of the fish and allowed the fly to come round into the slack where the trout was feeding.

Strangely, although I knew I wanted to move the fly I had to force myself to do it because it was alien to my normal dry-fly fishing practice. But as the fly approached the fish I steeled myself against the inbred instincts which told me not to, and twitched the rod tip. A few rings came from the otherwise inert offering, up came that trout and seized it, ignoring a dead natural drifting close by. That fish was a typically bullish brown trout, it lacked the speed of the rainbow but made up for it in brute strength and cunning. I eventually netted it and it weighed 3lb 10oz (1.5kg). The occasion hammered one point home: all trout do not behave in the same way; one can act differently from others nearby that are all behaving uniformly.

A mayfly hatch was the scene of a similar situation and again the trout were rising round me in great numbers but would not take my offerings. I studied one fish in particular and after a time I realized that it was not taking spent mayfly but the nymphs as they emerged at the surface.

I looked down into the pool and could see the nymphs as they spiralled up from the stream bed, then watched as a trout charged up from below and took a nymph as it struggled to shake free from the shock and emerge as the graceful insect we see dancing above the water. There always seems a certain sad finality to the mayfly event because its life is so short and it is unable to continue to give so much pleasure.

However, it was an irrefutable fact that on that day the trout preferred the hatching nymph, imitations of which were hard to obtain. But I did have a miniature Muddler Minnow which I greased up and fished inertly as if it were a dry fly, even though the Muddler did not move about as the struggling nymphs did. The fish recognized it as a hatching mayfly and trout were soon in the basket.

These instances and others like them have taught me to take my time when flyfishing and to stop and think when I feel I am doing it all correctly, but not catching fish and then blaming it on the trout. Some understanding of the trout's usual – and unusual – activities often helps to eliminate frustration and produce a relaxing and enjoyable day's fishing.

I have never used a dropper while dry-fly fishing, mainly because it is not practicable but more usually because it is not allowed on most waters I have visited. A dropper on the cast will preclude that presentation of the fly which is so essential when dry-fly fishing.

UPSTREAM NYMPH FISHING

This method is the most deadly of all for catching trout. If a nymph is correctly presented and fished it can seem to urge the trout into taking. But upstream nymphing is not allowed on many waters, particularly some chalksteams and on others it is allowed only in the latter half of the season when the fish have become more difficult after the mayfly hatch is past.

Although there may be times when the trout are rising freely, the fish often prefer to feed deeper on nymphs, corixae or shrimps. It can be at any depth and although I have had most trout on nymphs on the bottom, some have been taken from just below the surface. These slightly sub-surface fish give themselves away by the swirl they leave as they turn away after chasing and taking the insects.

The tackle for upstream nymphing is the same as that for the dry fly. It is not necessary to fish with a large fly, for accuracy of the presentation is what matters. Trout behave differently in differ-

Cast sufficiently far upstream that the fly can sink to the correct depth when it reaches the trout.

ent surroundings; in a deep pool where the current moves slowly at the lower level the fish roam about feeding casually. Sometimes they make a dash up through the water, but mostly they stay deep.

In streamy water where there is not a lot of cover the trout is prone to dart after food; but with weedy areas the fish stay in one place and allow the weed to channel the food towards them, and these trout are very challenging when sought with the dry fly. In the kind of situations described above all the fish have reacted very much in the same manner.

My line preference for nymph fishing is weight-forward and I have never used a dropper. The upstream nymph method allows the fly to be worked at depths which otherwise would be unfishable.

Drag does not present such a problem when nymph fishing as it does with the dry fly because trout are conditioned to their food darting about under the surface, and it is this normal action that we are trying to imitate and little movement of the artificial can be advantageous.

Top *A hooked fish battles upstream of the angler on this Montana creek. When first hooked, a trout will try to bolt for cover, and will also try to go downstream. However, the best position for the fisherman is downstream of the fish, because then he will be helped by the current, rather than hindered by it. Once the fish has been played out, its head can be lifted, and it can be carried into the waiting net by the current.*
Left *Bob Church nets a fighting rainbow on the River Test to help England on the way to winning the 1987 World Fly Fishing Championships.*

There are two ways of detecting the take when upstream fishing with the nymph. It is not done by feel as is usually the case, but by visual contact either with the fly or the leader. The trout can often be observed taking the fly but on most occasions it is necessary to concentrate intently on the point where the leader enters the water.

A take by the trout is telegraphed to the line by a twitch of the leader or a momentary dead stop, or the leader shooting forward for an inch or two. The strike should be made firmly and if the message from the trout was read correctly the fish should be hooked every time. In this style of fishing total concentration is as important as presentation.

The most notable fish I ever caught on a nymph was taken at dusk while I was fishing a small stream where there was a deep, dark pool beneath a low bridge. The water flowing beneath was swift, so in order to get the fly down deep to the fishing depth it had to be weighted and cast accurately under the bridge as far as possible.

As usual, there were brambles trailing from the bridge, for nothing is ever easy on this water, but it is always enjoyable fishing. There was another problem, too, in the shape of a large boulder in the pool which tended to snag any flies even slightly off course. It was nearly dark as I cast a weighted shrimp-pattern as far under the bridge as I could, but I was not able to see if it was a good cast, it seemed all right. Then I saw the line coming back down on the current, so I knew that I had not snagged the brambles.

Then the end of the fly line gave a slight, indeterminate movement and more from instinct than anything else I struck, and the resistance was solid and unmistakeable. The trout was determined and strong and could have taken me a long way downstream if it had gone that way, but it stayed in the deep pool and we just slugged it out. It was dark by the time I managed to slip the net under the fish, a perfect and beautiful wild brown trout of over 3lb (1.3kg).

Taking a long look at the fish, I slipped it back beneath the black, oily surface as it swirled past. I looked into that pool many times afterwards, and fished it, but I never saw that trout again.

In my opinion it is more essential to have a long leader when nymph fishing than it is with other aritficials because if the water is deep and slow the line could be directly over the fish and the nymph hanging beneath it. This obviously has to be avoided and a long leader helps to do so. I prefer to know that the line has gone a long way over the fish before the nymph arrives. It also takes the angle out of the line that a short leader will create and in so doing enables a much more direct strike when a trout takes.

Even though the fly will be sunk and the fish deeper in the water than when dry-fly fishing it is still very important to use stealth and watercraft. The refraction of light in the water can reveal the angler to the fish, which does not work the other way round, so a cautious approach, as always, is necessary.

When fishing deep, I prefer to cast directly

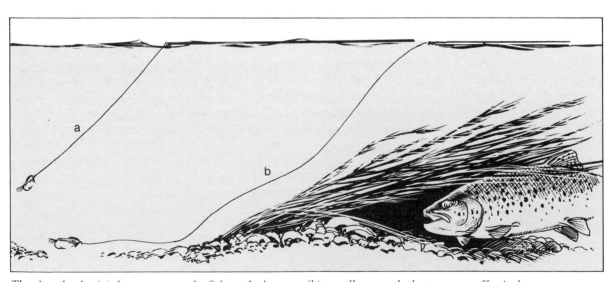

The short leader (a) does not cover the fish on the bottom; (b) trundles over the bottom very effectively.

upstream, especially if a bend in the river or stream allows a cast in that direction. This is because a take is detected much more easily and the straight line between you and the fish means that the strike is near-instantaneous and very effective. Line should be retrieved at the same rate as the current is bringing it towards you, but you must keep bends out of the line.

Once the cast has been completed the fly should be lifted smoothly from the water, but watch for any pursuing trout that may well make a last-second snatch of the fly at the surface. If a fish does this it is usually with severity and will turn down again quickly, so if you hold the fish then you might well 'bounce' it off the fly. The rod tip has instantly to be lowered a fraction so that the trout can turn without meeting resistance, which should come when its head is down. Then, the hook will be pulled into a firm hold on the jaw.

Now to the situation where one is fishing a deep hole where the current is even. The fly to select will be of sufficient weight to take it to the bottom quickly enough to enable the entire bottom of the hole to be fished. If the shelf of the pool is gradual the weight can be less than is needed when there is a steep ledge where a fly with weight can send the fish dashing off unless the artificial was fished with grace. In fact, flies with a lot of metal are to be avoided because there is little pleasure in fishing with them. Of course, there are pools that require a fly to be thrown in rather than cast, but the situation is relative and if a fly is selected that carries relatively less weight than a larger one it

has less resistance in the water and will sink at the same rate as a heavier one.

A big fly is not necessary, for colour can be the attractor. I have one fly that I use with unfailing success on all of my expeditions to small streams, it is the Shrimp pattern that Richard Walker devised, with a minor adaptation or two of my own. The lead on this fly is tied along the back of the hook-shank, making the fly fish upside-down, which gives it terrific hooking reliability.

If the water deepens gradually, casting the fly well upstream will not only give the fly time to sink, it will also allow the line to be straightened in readiness for the all-important detection of the take. The fly should be allowed to fish over the stream-bed without interference because I have seen trout in a deep pool scatter and panic when a fly has trundled past them, then one will suddenly dash forward and take it, but from their original panic I would not have anticipated hooking one. This behaviour has been repeated a number of times in the same pool and I have always had a few fish from it.

When a heavy fly is used it sometimes has to be assisted in its way across the stream-bed by means of a slow retrieve at about the same speed as the upper current. This can provoke a take by triggering off an instinctive reaction strike which is often too fast to hook the fish.

The attraction of the fly in these deep pools is probably due to the fact that, because there is little current where the fish are lying, the line, being moved by the upper current, in turn carries

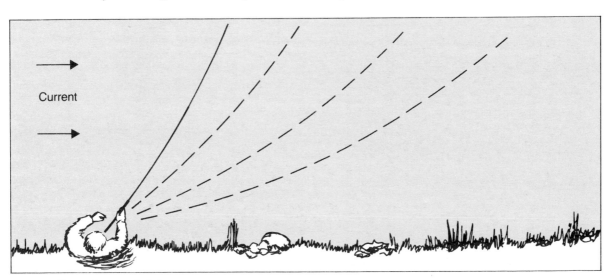

Retrieve line at the speed of the current.

Left *An angler fishes a river in low-water conditions in fading light.*
Above *Fishing upstream on a brook where wading provides an unrestricted back-cast.*

---

the fly past the trout. This is in contrast to the movement of other natural food drifting about in the same area. The fish, and particularly rainbows, are impelled by hunger and instinct to chase and take the fly.

In areas which are immediately downstream of a hatch or mill-race, and where the bottom has been scoured out, the current will race over a deep hole which in its deepest part has little or no water movement. It may not be apparent to the casual eye but this is what is happening. On other occasions there will be eddies which provide other conflicting currents, and so in these streams there is a real hotch-potch of currents where trout will be lying.

To fish them, cast into the heaviest water and the fly will be caught in the turbulence and forced into deep water. The one thing to avoid is the line racing off and negating the assistance that the water has provided in sinking the fly. If the line lies on the surface between the swift water and the eddy it will drift more slowly and the fly will continue to sink.

If the presentation has been correct the fly will move around the bottom of the pool until the line is taken off downstream by the current. The interesting thing about fishing a lie of this kind is that no two casts ever appear to fish in the same way, and this is because the tumbling water is varying slightly all the time, both in strength and direction. Fish that are hooked in a pool like this rarely leave it in a downstream dash, but when they do the results are spectacular.

When trout are lying between weedbeds they do not normally move either side to take a fly, neither do they rise to one. Their vision appears to be fixed on the gap in the weed in the direction from where the food comes and they remain oblivious to anything else. So not only is accuracy in placing the fly essential but one must ensure

that it has sunk the correct depth before it reaches the trout, which are always right on the bottom.

It is very frustrating to watch as a fly moves past these fish again and again and they do not move an inch to take it. But the first time it is presented right on to their nose the mouth opens to reveal the white inside then closes firmly. The strike is made and the trout instantly twists, pulling the rod down and heading for the weedy sanctuary.

There have been times late in the season when I have been tempted to fish too fine for trout that had become 'educated', but I have paid for it in the most sorry fashion, to the degree where I will not fish with anything less than a 4lb (1.8kg) breaking strain leader, and more usually 6lb (2.7kg) as it provides the necessary stiffness.

One occasion which gave me grief occurred when I was fishing a nymph on a 2lb (0.9kg) leader, which is as light as I would go in open water where I can handle a trout easily on it. But on the day in question, because it was sunny and the fish shy, I used the light leader to trundle a fly between some weed at about 45 degrees to my position.

There was a definite take from a trout which I had not seen in the gin-clear water and I struck. The fish immediately took off to its right, under and through some steamer-weed, then leapt clear of the water showing itself to be an absolutely superb and sizeable brown trout. Then the leader parted in the weed. I could do nothing because I had been playing the weed and not the fish.

I abhor leaving hooks in fish, so now I only fish

A nymph tied to fish upside-down will ride over snags and has greater hooking potential.

when I am positive that I can play them without interference and bring them to the net. Rather than losing that beautiful trout in that way I would rather not have hooked it at all.

Fishing a nymph in open water requires a very different approach. To begin with, the fact that the water is open probably means that the surface is untroubled and so if you can see the fish be assured that they can see you, your profile will be obvious. I approach open water with more caution than I do a pool and always from downstream.

A trout that is in shallower water is more likely to chase a fly than one where the water is deeper, and the presence of more than one fish often leads them to compete for the offering, so if you can cover both your chances of hooking one are good. But remember that there are two pairs of eyes in the water and if the cast is clumsy both fish will be off.

I have cast to a single fish which moved off, then having followed it and waited until it stopped I cast again and caught it. This was a rare exception, for once a trout has been 'spooked' it is best left alone. It will eventually return to its feeding station and you can try again.

If a fly in open water can be seen by the fish it will be inspected closely, for the trout has stationed itself where it is because food which can be seen in the area is apprehended and taken.

152

Here, the depth of the fly is not crucial, and neither is the path that the fly takes. But these trout quickly detect a clumsy cast or a poor approach, so they are worth catching and usually put up a spirited fight, running and leaping before they give themselves up to the net.

There are times when the trout can be seen bulging at the surface. This bulge is caused by a trout turning under the surface as he takes a nymph. Some people mistake this for a rise to a dry fly, but careful observation will reveal that the fish never actually breaks the surface. This is the time to try for him with a nymph, either weighted or unweighted, depending on the depth of the water and the strength of the current. The strength of the current has also to be taken into consideration in the presentation of the fly. It must be remembered that the bulge which gives away the station of the fish will be carried downstream by the current, so the presentation of the nymph must be upstream from the first sign of the bulge and far enough up so that the fly will be at the required working depth by the time it arrives at the trout's position. A long leader is essential for upstream nymphing so that the fly line is well back from the fish by the time the nymph is with him. In many cases the fish will be feeding hard on the bottom of the stream, so it will be necessary to ensure that the nymph is presented at that level. A nymph that is off the bottom will very often be ignored. To this end I usually use a weighted nymph, although I have on occasions resorted to pinching on a split shot at the head of the fly.

The idea is to allow the current to carry the fly down to the trout in a very natural way. An acceptable alternative is to retrieve at a speed slightly quicker than the current so that the fly moves along the bottom and attacts the trout's attention that way.

Natural movement by the fly is even more important in a dead water situation, where there is little or no current to move the fly about. The answer, usually, is to cast across and slightly upstream and retrieve the fly fairly quickly. As soon as the trout sees the fly he is more likely to snatch at it than ignore it. This is rather similar to fishing in still water, but for some reason the trout in streams respond very eagerly to a stripped nymph.

INDUCED TAKE

The principle of the induced take is simple and the technique is quite deadly once it has been mastered. It occurs in all trout fishing but the angler is not always aware of having used it because he has not seen the nearby trout.

If you can see the trout you should be able to induce that fish to take the fly by moving it away. This movement makes it irresistible to the fish, which chases and takes it. That is the induced take and I have caught many trout and grayling that way. In practice it might take several passes at the fish with the fly before the trout takes, for the one essential, as usual, is that the fish must not be aware of the angler for if it sees him it will be off long before the fly can be cast.

It is possible to induce a trout to take in any depth of water and the current speed is also immaterial, for I have induced takes in shallow, swift-running water as well as in deep, slow water: the main essential is timing.

You may see trout rising and feeding, or feel that there are unseen trout in the area; sometimes an overhanging bank or bush forces a situation where the trout is just out of sight from the fishing position but has been seen from another view-point and marked. This makes a particularly

Right *The vegetation left after cutting provided the angler with cover when stalking this spirited trout.*
Below *The induced take:*
(a) entry; (b) sinking to required depth; (c) fishing into the trout's vision; (d) lifting the fly away induces the fish to take.

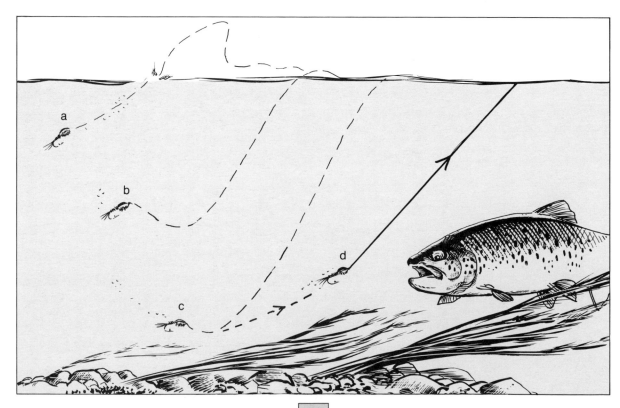

exciting moment when your fly comes into view and then the unseen trout rockets up to take it.

But it is better to be able to see the fish and one lying in open water will usually be feeding, for a resting or 'hiding' trout does not remain in the open to be seen. Cast the fly in the normal way and allow it to pass the fish without it being moved in case the trout takes it, but if it ignores the artificial or shows just a flicker of interest the induced take should be tried.

I always use a nymph for this and the weight (or lack of it) depends entirely on the current where the fish is lying. If the water is deep it does not mean that the fly should be heavily leaded. With a slow current a lightly leaded fly is preferable. Trout are occasionally taken on the soft 'plop' which a fly makes as it hits the water but I prefer to assume that this will not happen so I cast well upstream with a lighter fly and let it drift down to the fish as it sinks. This makes a natural presentation of the fly if the fish has the fly in view, especially if the current is affecting it.

There are too many warning signs if a heavily leaded fly makes a splash as it enters the water near a trout, then sinks like a stone. In my opinion, a more leisurely and sedate presentation will stand much more of a chance of succeeding.

If the trout has already ignored the fly, offer it again, and let it pass the fish at the correct level, but as it nears the trout the rod should be lifted with a smooth, flowing motion which raises the fly in the water and away from the fish. In theory, if the trout is feeding, the fly will be greedily snatched before it is inspected. The fly might be ignored again and again but so long as it does not see the angler it will eventually take the fly and the angler will have that wonderful thrill of achievement.

The correct moment to start the upward movement of the fly depends upon the current, but trout must be given the chance to see the fly as it comes to them and then, while it is still in full view, the fly should be swept upwards and away. The trout will often turn and chase it, so fish the fly right up to the surface before making the next cast. It is important to be able to see the fish so that one can gauge its reactions when it has not taken the fly, because several abortive attempts might reveal that it reacted more strongly to the fly coming from one direction, and a decision can be made accordingly.

One certain thing is that it does not matter how accurate the presentation is if something else alerts the trout, and one thing that does this is the sun which casts the angler's shadow on the water or causes the fly line or leader to glint.

Whenever a fly is to be fished sinking, rub the leader with mud to help remove the shine and aid its sinking. There are several proprietary brands of leader treatments which do this but ordinary waterside mud works surprisingly well in degreasing line.

On streams and rivers I always fish from a downstream position when trying to induce takes because this tactic is always carried out at close quarters and it is important to be out of sight of the fish before the fly is moved. I do not know if it works from upstream, but it does on stillwaters where I should have been in full view of the trout. The fact is that once a fish has been triggered to take the fly it will continue the action even if you are in full view of the fish as it turns towards you; the only thing that stops it will be a too quick reaction and a sharp movement.

If the trout is intent on a take it will get to the fly before it leaves the water, but make sure before you strike that the white inside of its mouth first shows, then the jaws close firmly. This tactic is reliant on visual contact and accuracy of presentation so I use a fly which can be seen easily in the water and which I have confidence in.

A nymph such as a Pheasant Tail with a coloured thorax, or a leaded Shrimp, are two of my favourites. But at times the favourites can be totally ignored and you might feel that the fish are not interested. It has happened to me many times, and I take up the challenge, searching through the fly box for a pattern that will provoke a take.

At times I have ended up fishing 'blind', unable to see the fly and then only instinct and the reaction of the trout will tell you when to strike. The reward then is to see that dark shape transformed into a twisting, flashing demon as the hook is driven home and the rod springs to life.

The induced take can be successful on any type of water and under any circumstances. It relies for its success on the principle that the fly is presented correctly and the trout is interested in the offering. The greed or excitement of the trout is then triggered by the removal – or attempted removal – of the fly from the trout's field of activity. As long as the trout has confidence in the offering it will do all that it can to eat it.

On small stillwaters, the induced take is the

main weapon in the armoury of those that stalk large trout in the clear waters.

There is always a huge degree of satisfaction in duping a trout into taking the fly, and we all do this on reservoirs when we cast a fly at a rising fish and then move it. On rivers and streams the excitement is enhanced by the fact that there is also the current and the clarity of the water to contend with. However, the idea of working a sunken fly across dead water is really also a form of induced take. The water does not have to be moving to cause the method to be effective.

The most difficult trout to induce are those that lie in shallow water. For a start, there is not enough depth of water to give the trout plenty of time to see it as it rises through the water. There is also the problem that trout lying in shallow water are able to see much more clearly what goes on around them – in this case, a rod that is false casting and a line that is flashing through the air. The disturbance that the fly creates on its entry into the water is another problem to contend with. If there is any sun on the water it is probably as well to forget that fish altogether and look for others in deeper water. Sun on the water will also cause the leader to glint sufficiently to alert the trout, and will cause a shadow which will, again, alert the fish. If the fish is lying in shade, however, it is a different matter entirely. There is then only the matter of presentation to contend with.

In shallower water it is preferable to approach the trout with the utmost caution up to the point where you are almost abreast of him, and then still to keep the lowest profile possible. And bear in mind that a fish that is feeding avidly is usually far easier to approach than one that is simply lying at rest.

It is necessary to give the fish a clear view of the fly, as always when inducing. I have found that it is almost always better to present the fly well upstream of the fish and leave it to drift down to him, but possibly moving a little quicker than the current. The rod should always be held high in order to keep as much line off the surface as possible in view of the slight depth of the water. It will be necessary to start to take the fly away from the fish earlier than if the water were deeper. The rod, by this time, should be lowered to decrease the angle of the exit of the fly from the water, and it is necessary to speed up the retrieve of the line as the rod tip is dropped in order to compensate for any slack that might occur. By this time the fly line will have passed the fish, and so will not be a hindrance.

If causing the inducement from upstream of the fish does not work, it may be possible to reach a satisfactory presentation from a different angle.

For obvious reasons I usually prefer to present the fly to the trout upstream of him, or slightly closer to the near bank than his station. To touch the fish with the line would be disastrous. When the fish is in shallow water, however, and has refused an offering which has come from directly upstream, it might be possible to induce him to take from across the stream.

This is really a last resort, as the fish is given so much time to see the tackle, but I have successfully induced many trout from across the stream. The object is to cast beyond the fish and upstream, and as the fly is brought down on the current to retrieve it across the stream so that it passes in front of his nose. As it does so and continues on downstream behind him, the fish will often turn without warning, almost as if he is in flight, chase the fly and grab it. In this case the fly is not so much brought through the water and up, as retrieved in the manner of a stripped retrieve. Because the fly ends up at one's feet, the excitement of hooking a trout this way can be almost overwhelming.

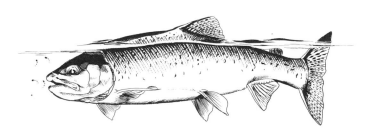

WET-FLY FISHING

In rivers and streams wet-fly fishing is the simplest form of trout fishing. The object of presentation of the wet fly is to imitate an insect struggling with the current, so it is fished across and downstream. In slack water it can be fished very much the same way as wet-fly fishing in stillwater because some movement has to be given to the artificial to attract the attention of the trout.

The patterns for wet-fly fishing are the traditional ones that have been used on lochs, loughs, rivers and streams for decades and they are as deadly today as they ever were. The cast consists of three or four flies as in loch-style fishing and usually includes an attractor but not a buoyant bob-fly. One does not want to skate the fly or create a wake because this will betray the presence of the tackle, and because the current will be pulling against the tackle, the top dropper will be near the surface.

On rough streams small flies tied spider fashion will outfish almost any other pattern and yet do not produce other than modest results when fished on similar waters elsewhere.

On many waters, fishing a wet fly downstream can be very effective, and on larger rivers it is the best way to effectively cover the water. The style is not allowed on all waters and if there are any rules laid down for a fishery, particularly in England, it is quite possible that this method is forbidden. This of course does not indicate that it is the most efficient method on a water but if the fishery is well stocked it takes more fish than any other style when carried out correctly.

Where it is allowed on a water and practised by a good number of anglers the trout quickly become 'educated' to it (as they do to all other methods) so it requires just as much thought and skill as any other method.

Tactics and Technique
The secret is to present the flies to the fish so that the tackle is not evident in the form of wake or knots. Here, one should have a leader as long as can be managed, with the first dropper well down the cast so that the floating line is commonly used as the angler makes his way downstream, but there are few occasions where a slow-sinking line or a sink-tip line might be more appropriate. The rate of sink of the fly depends on whether or not it is weighted (which is not usual) and whether the flies are fished as they enter the water.

Right *This broad stretch of the River Wharfe, Yorkshire, provides excellent scope for fishing down with a wet fly.* Below *The gravel bar provides a pool behind it and increases the pace of the current to the side.*

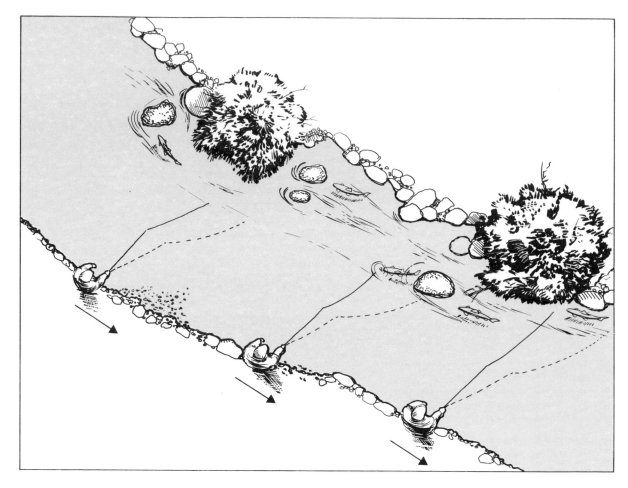

The cast is made across and downstream and if the line is held fast in the hand immediately, the flies will start to swing across the current but they will be fishing higher in the water than if the line were allowed to drift for a short distance before it was held and fished. Mending the line upstream will also have the same effect.

It is better to allow the flies to travel a short distance first so that they will sink and as soon as they are down they will swing with the current and across to a position downstream of the angler. It is here where many takes come, the trout having followed the fly across, and as it stops its swing it sinks.

But if the flies are allowed to do this the trout will probably lose interest and so some retrieve has to be made exactly when the flies reach the end of their travel, which makes it similar to an induced take.

The advantage of fishing a downstream wet fly is that much more water can be covered very

By moving quietly downstream at short intervals, all likely lies will be covered.

efficiently and it is also a very relaxing way of fishing and the angler can enjoy the change of scenery as he works slowly downstream. It is not as exhausting as stalking individual trout, where great concentration is required in focussing on the water. At the same time it is an energetic style, requiring concentration in a different way because if you cannot see the fish then you cannot tell what its reactions are. You will have to try different flies until you find the right one.

There is tremendous enjoyment in fishing for those small, wild and very fast trout of moorland rivers with really small flies and light tackle with nothing but nature and the elements as your companions. These small fish are usually so fast that if you are inattentive they can rap the fly and be gone before you can strike.

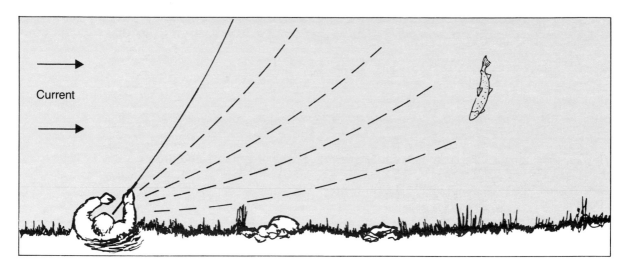

A fish may follow across the stream as the line progresses, finally taking near the bank.

As soon as any movement is detected on the fly line the fish should be struck because it will already be turning and away. A longer rod is an advantage on these waters because it can pick up more line off the water when the hook is set on the strike and it also helps in keeping control of the flies. If the rod tip is kept well out into the cast the flies can later be followed round slowly with the rod tip.

This allows you to 'hang' the flies in an area to which you want to give some attention. If the rod is pointed downstream as soon as the cast has begun, the flies will come round in the current much more quickly than if the rod were used to work them. It is not a method I have tried, but I have seen anglers lifting the rod-tip with a quivering motion which presumably makes the flies dance in the water. At the right time this 'quivering' method could probably take more fish than simply allowing the flies to swing round, but it catches fish and so must be worth consideration.

Lies

The trout of course will be lying where they always are but because the flies are sunk the means of fishing for them is a little different. Slack water and eddies are best fished from the slack-water side, the cast being made into the faster water and the flies allowed to swing round into the quieter area.

Flies do not swing far into slack water and the retrieve should be made along the edge between it and the faster water. This is where the trout are conditioned to expect food and so the artificials can also be recognized as edible and taken. Slack water is usually in the form of a pool and the first cast ought to swing into the head, followed by another.

But to stay there and keep casting will disturb the trout, so it is wise to take a step downstream after two casts and repeat the action. If the pool is not very large the alternative is to make each cast a little longer, which will cover the area and any trout that has not risen on previous casts might take as the fly comes to it from behind.

In slack water, this method works equally well from a downstream position and though it requires hard work, in faster water the flies can be retrieved more quickly than the current. This use of the current forces the flies deeper in the water.

For all trout fishing the absence of sunlight is an advantage and as the flies are being fished at the depth where the trout are lying, it means that there is a greater chance of avoiding tell-tale shadows or glitter from the tackle. In flowing or stillwater, fish whenever possible with the sun behind you and keep low so that the fly is presented to the trout while coming out of the sun and appears as a silhouette. If the sun is in the angler's eyes it will be behind the trout and the fly will show more shape and colour. The best chances of success are in the morning, before the sun touches the water and then after it has set; and fishing in shaded areas gives the angler much more chance.

WEATHER EFFECTS

The weather has a large effect on trout fishing in rivers. In cooler seasons the trout become sluggish and drop into the deeper areas, venturing into the shallows only on sunnier days and if the river suddenly receives an influx of water, from whatever cause, the fishing will be affected.

In summer, more water is not necessarily affected by temperature to the degree where the fish will stop feeding, but there may well be an introduction of colour, or perhaps chemicals used in farming, into what was a previously clear stream and while it may not be harmful it will unsettle the trout.

In these days of abstraction and 'efficiency' it is sad that all lowland rivers now suffer from severe fluctuation in water level, and in quantity and quality. It seems that no sooner has a river in an arable area received an injection of fresh water than it loses it and is back down to its previous low level.

Abstraction has stopped the back-up effect from the sea that used to occur and this is supposed to be beneficial because the water quickly becomes fishable again, but I am still to be convinced that coloured water, except when it is harmful, will put all the fish off their feed. And we know that a hint of colour is good because it helps our approach to the water and hides our tackle from the trout for the short time that can make the difference between catching or frightening them off.

It is sometimes said that fish will feed if the air pressure is dropping, but are less inclined to do so if the air pressure is rising. A rising glass usually accompanies better weather, even sunshine, in which case the fish will be inclined to lie deeper. In periods of prolonged sunshine (days and weeks, not just one day or several hours) the fish most certainly retreat to deeper water in lakes, lochs and reservoirs. And in streams and rivers they will find a deep pool so that they have some respite from the sun, as long as the water has sufficient oxygen to sustain them. It it does, they may be inclined to carry on feeding.

The impending arrival of a thunderstorm, or other conditions when the air becomes very heavy and still, will cause the fish to change their feeding pattern suddenly. They may go off the feed altogether.

When the air becomes still and heavy, fly presentation becomes harder, especially with a dry fly. The air forces the fly onto the water much quicker than normal, and this often results in tangles.

In rivers and streams, the trout are not able to escape the atrocities and anomalies of the weather in so easy a fashion as their stillwater brethren, so they have to suffer the consequences. However, they are able to move away from certain areas that are uncomfortable. On cooler days in early and late season, it would be inadvisable to seek fish near to a tributary which was introducing cool water. In the summer, the same tributary would bring welcome oxygen into the stream and the fish might well congregate close to it provided that it was not too dirty or tainted.

Whatever the weather, it is unlikely to keep flyfishermen indoors, unless it be by a warm fire on those bitter early-season days, and there is very little that we can do under most conditions other than to adapt our approach to fit in with the weather. However, it is vitally important to cease fishing when there is thunder and lightning about. I am sure that most, if not all, flyfishers are aware that carbon fibre and other modern materials are excellent lightning conductors, and this should never be forgotten. During a thunderstorm, lay the rod down and retire to a strategic position.

The end of the battle on a small stream.

FLIES FOR RIVERS AND STREAMS

The flies which are used for fishing in rivers and streams vary considerably from river to river and from area to area.

For instance, on the moorland rocky streams, the 'spider' type flies tend to be very popular, whilst on the slower and broader rivers, the more heavily dressed wet flies and dry flies seem to be the order of the day.

A sparsely-dressed spider type of fly will sink more quickly and have more movement, and this is probably the reason why they are more effective on the minor, swifter streams. The fly is in the water for a shorter time and therefore has to be used to good effect. On the broader waters, where a long cast is more normal, the trout have more time to see and follow the fly, so some integral parts of its dressing which deceive or attract the trout are most important.

In wet-fly fishing, a spider hackle can be very effective on some days.

I was fishing alone at the foot of the Pennine Peaks in Izaac Walton country and the trout were not altogether obliging. The mayfly was over and there was not much of anything else hatching. The water was gin clear and the bailiff had informed me that I was allowed to fish any way I chose with a fly. On a slow pool I drifted a mayfly beneath overhanging branches: nothing. I was retrieving the fly hurriedly when the line suddenly tightened to my hand and raising my split cane 'wand', I was into a brown trout. Drifting the mayfly downstream and retrieving it then produced fish so monotonously that the day would have been spoilt had I continued. It did prove, however, that there were many fish in the river, and this encouraged me to renew my efforts with the nymph and dry fly, with better results.

Since then I have found that a hackled fly retrieved across dead water or held in the current will catch fish if they are there to be caught. The softer hackles, such as guinea fowl (which are usually rather large) or partridge, are the most effective ones. Ordinary hen hackles can be effective if they are soft enough, and they produce a plain effect that can be very desirable, especially on a dull day when the fly should appear more solid.

I normally prefer a dry fly to float in the surface film rather than to ride high on the surface. However, during rather prolific hatches of, for instance, olives and other ephemerids, which only dent the water with their feet, it can sometimes be desirable to have the fly riding high in common with the naturals around it.

There are many experiments that can be carried out with flies in river fishing, but I would advise that the size and basic outline of the fly must conform to the natural which is being taken (if there is a hatch). The colour of the fly may not be so crucial, especially if the light is not good.

Above *Freshwater shrimp; trout get their pink flesh from feeding on these.*
Top right *The size and outline of a dry fly should conform to the natural being taken.*
Right *A small wild brown trout taken from a stream.*

164

NYMPHS

Copper Wire Pheasant-tail

One of the first flies that I tried and which has always proved highly successful. Basically it is a simple Pheasant-tail Nymph but copper wire is used in place of tying silk and the pheasant tail fibres are twisted round the copper wire as it is tied. The thorax is built up with the copper wire, which also gives weight and visibility, making it an excellent fly for the induced-take method. The sizes should be kept small, which helps to make a neater and therefore more presentable fly.

Leaded Shrimp

The exact pattern described earlier. I have used it in standard green or brown, but have found that by far the most successful colours are amber and orange.

Pheasant-tail Nymphs

In general these are very adaptable and can be tied in various sizes, materials and colours. Chenille can be used for the body and it is better on large flies because it gives bulk. I have also used peacock herl and feathers from my African grey parrot, plus others, all of which have proved successful.

Corixa

A simple tying which I designed after a day on a river when the fish were feeding just below the surface and would not take anything I offered. When I used this fly on subsequent occasions when the fish were behaving in the same way it worked very well. The body is unweighted and the material is white chenille ribbed with fine silver wire. The back is formed by pulling over pheasant tail fibres of the correct length so that they can be formed underneath the fly and left untrimmed to form the legs. This fly has only worked for me on slower water.

Claret Nymph

Another nymph which I tied to give visibility while incorporating materials attractive to trout. I have usually used a heavy wire hook and eliminated the weight, although it does catch fish when slightly leaded. The body is dubbed claret seal's fur ribbed with red copper wire and immediately behind the head is a ruff of spun white deer's hair for visibility. The head is then finished in black varnish. This fly seems more attractive to brown trout than to rainbows.

Damselfly Nymph

The stream version of this nymph can be slightly smaller than the stillwater version, and I prefer the rougher, more traditional dressing. I use the Captain Hamilton short-shank hook with heavy wire. As with all nymphs, I tie it in different weights. The use of lead foil from wine bottles, cut into strips and laid along the shank, allows for versatility as any number of strips can be used.

In all cases, the lead should be tied along the length of the hook before the pattern is started. The position of the lead, whether along the back of the hook shank or the underside, will affect the way that the fly fishes. I resist the temptation to wind the lead around the hook shank because it can hardly ever be wound so perfectly that the fly fishes evenly.

The hook sizes for this fly are 12 or 10. A bunch of olive cock hackle fibres are used to create the tail fibres, olive seal fur is used for the body, dubbed on sparsely to keep a slim outline. A palmered olive cock hackle runs the length of the body and is trimmed back to create stubs. The thorax is built up from the seal fur, and a couple of turns around the back of the eye with the body hackle finish off the fly. This hackle is forced to slope back by the finishing of the head.

A fine catch of brown trout.

Hare's Ear Nymph

This is one pattern that catches many fish on all types of water, and I have taken many river trout on it. The hook sizes are again small: 12, 14 or 16 on a Captain Hamilton. The tail is furnace cock hackle fibres, and the body and thorax are made from the fur taken from a hare's ear or mask. This is dubbed onto the tying silk and then shaped to build up the tapered body and thorax. Some dark feather fibres are used to form wing cases over the thorax and the main body only is ribbed with oval gold tinsel.

The use of lead in this dressing is optional. However, a leaded version is best when the induced take is being tried.

Stonefly Nymph

I have tied this pattern using latex. If you have yet to try this material, I would recommend without hesitation that you do so. It can be a little difficult to handle until one is used to it, but the trick is to remember to stretch it (not too hard) as it is tied. The segmented-body effect that it gives to nymphs is very realistic indeed.

I usually tie this on a long-shank 12 or 14 Partridge bucktail streamer hook. Two bronze mallard feather fibres, not too long, form the tail. The body is then created with brown latex in a basic nymph shape, and a thorax of dark seal fur is built up. Then latex is stretched over this to form a shell-back. Legs of knotted feather fibres are built into the thorax and left short. I use heron feathers for this. The thorax and head are then coated with clear varnish.

Again, the basic nymph shape is used, and the latex gives a very lifelike impression. I tie it in a variety of colours, but always sombre ones. The introduction of a little orange or green seal fur with the main thorax dubbing can be effective.

Stick Fly

This pattern, tied exactly as for stillwater fishing, also produces trout in streams.

Marabou Nymph

I include this pattern because it is possible to experiment and produce a whole range of flies. It is tied on small long-shank hooks the same size as for the Stonefly, and it does not have a tail. It is possible to combine different colours of marabou to provide a realistic effect. I prefer to use brown, green and black, and occasionally orange.

The method of tying is to take a number of strands of marabou substitute and tie them in at the bend of the hook with a strand of gold oval tinsel. The whole rope of marabou fibres is then taken up to the thorax and tied off, whilst the tinsel is wound up to form a rib. A thorax is then formed with either fur, herl or the marabou, and wing cases are formed from pheasant tail fibres. The head hackle is tied in false, and I usually use olive cock hackle fibres for this.

Amber Nymph

This is the same pattern as used on stillwaters, and will take fish when the sedge flies are on the water.

There are many ways of experimenting with nymph patterns. However, I am most satisfied if they have a rough outline. Seal fur is used quite extensively on nymphs, but I would recommend the use of other furs and hair as well. Wool can be very effective, but it always seems to give an uneven outline. The best way of preventing this is to separate it into strands before beginning to work with it. The smaller strands are more manageable and the bulk can be built up to the desired effect.

Hair and rabbit fur are useful materials with all types of flies, and nymphs are no exception to this.

I always ensure that I have plenty of tinsels to hand, and I must confess to a preference for gold tinsel in order that they are sombre in colour. This is because most river insects seem to have a distinct preference for immaculate camouflage, therefore I want my flies to be noticeable but not overtly obvious.

There are many more patterns available to the flyfisher in specialist books. The selection I have included here will provide all of the basic shapes that the trout comes across regularly in his environment. The colours and sizes can be inter-changed to give almost any desired effect, and modern fly-tying materials make experimentation easy. I would strongly recommend anyone tying his own nymphs for streams and rivers not to be tempted to tie them too large. It is much better to offer the fish a small, well-tied fly than to thrust an outsized offering into his environment, making him take fright immediately. And this same result can also be caused by the use of too much colour or flash in the fly.

A fisherman waits for a take, having cast to a likely-looking spot.

WET FLIES

Partridge and Orange
This is a traditional spider-type pattern. It is very simple to tie. The sizes are small: 12, 14 or 16. The body, traditionally, is orange floss silk but I often tie it with orange seal fur with a close rib of oval gold tinsel to keep the body outline neat. The hackle is spun brown partridge and the head forces it to slope gently backwards.

Partridge and Green
This is exactly the same pattern as above, with a green body.

Partridge and Black
This version has a black body.

Ke-He
This spider pattern is a little more involved. It is inclined to come to the surface, but the addition of a limited amount of weight can prevent this. Originally a loch fly, it will also catch fish on rivers when fished with a team of flies. The body is bronze peacock herl, and it has a tail of golden pheasant tippet with a splash of red wool. The red wool could be tied as a tag in front of the tail. The hackle is brown cock hackle wound behind the eye and tied to slope backwards.

Zulu
This, again, is traditionally a loch fly but I have taken fish on it in small sizes – 14 and 16 on rivers and streams.

The body is black wool or dubbed seal fur ribbed with flat, fine silver tinsel. A black cock hackle is palmered the length of the body. Again, this fly has a tendency to rise to the surface and if drag is to be avoided it should be fished carefully.

Black and Peacock Spider
This pattern is tied in exactly the same fashion as the stillwater version.

March Brown Spider
Prolific hatches of the March Brown do not occur on too many waters these days, but the fly still catches fish on all types of water. The body of this fly is medium brown seal fur ribbed with fine silver wire. The tail is several brown cock hackle fibres and the head is spun speckled partridge hackle.

Winged Pheasant-tail
This is a simple wet fly. The body is pheasant tail fibres, roped together, shaped and ribbed with gold, oval tinsel. The wings are woodcock slips, traditionally, but if this is not available there are several acceptable substitutes. This fly is given a false hackle of furnace cock hackle fibres.

June Fly
This is a pattern Bob Church tied originally for stillwaters, but I have taken fish on it on lochs and rivers. It is representative of an Olive. A gold tag is tied at the rear of the fly, and the rest of the body is pale olive seal fur or wool. The wings are grey starling or similar, and there is a hackle of furnace cock tied behind the eye and sloping backwards.

March Brown
This pattern works well on all types of waters.

The tail is light partridge fibres, the body grey rabbit or seal fur dubbed and ribbed with fine gold oval tinsel or wire. The wings are hen pheasant centre feather slips, and there is a hackle of dark partridge, either false or spun and tied to slope back.

Mallard and Claret
This pattern is the same as that tied for stillwaters and is an excellent catcher of fish.

Peter Ross
I have had more success with this fly on rivers

An Orkney brown trout.

than on stillwaters.

The rear half of the body is flat silver tinsel and the front half red seal fur ribbed with oval silver tinsel. The wings are teal flank feathers, and a black cock hackle is tied false at the throat.

Black Pennell

This is an easily tied fly which catches trout on all waters. The tail is simply a few golden pheasant tippets, and the body is black floss silk or seal fur ribbed with silver tinsel. The hackle is a long black cock hackle spun behind the eye of the hook and left to stand out.

Invicta

I would never be without this pattern when the sedges are about, whatever type of trout fishing I am engaged in. It is an immensely successful pattern wherever it is fished.

The tail is a few fibres of golden pheasant crest feather and the body is yellow (golden) seal fur ribbed with gold oval tinsel. The body is palmered with a ginger cock hackle and there is a false hackle at the thoat of blue jay. The wings are hen pheasant centre tail. This fly is more of an attractor than an imitator or deceiver, but it is very effective.

Silver Invicta

This pattern is the same as for the stillwater fly. It is identical to the Invicta apart from the fact that the body is flat silver tinsel.

I tie my own wet flies, but have not deviated from any of the traditional patterns to an extent where they have become personalized versions. For stream and river fishing, the traditional patterns are still the best by a very long way and the tyings are freely available. Local knowledge will reveal the best patterns for any water and observation of the fly life will indicate which patterns will be effective on any given day. The patterns in my box are mostly small and dark or drab and I always have a variety of spider patterns which are so important for fishing for brown trout on waters that are not as rich in food as chalkstreams.

Making oneself inconspicuous by standing well back from the water's edge reduces the likelihood of scaring the fish.

DRY FLIES

Having experimented with a number of dry fly tyings of my own I have turned full circle and returned to the traditional flies – with the exception of one. Neither parachute hackle flies nor no-hackle flies have given me as much success as the old standbys such as the Olives and Sherry Spinners, Grey Wulff, Tupps Indispensable, Coachman and others. It is very important to have a large selection of dry flies because size is of paramount importance and so also is the natural insect on which the trout are feeding. You must be able to match as near as possible the hatch that is occurring.

Rough Olive

Blue-winged Olive

Dark Olive

Tupps Indispensable

Grey Wulff

Olive Dun

Dark Mayfly

I do use other Mayfly patterns but this is one that I adapted from an article in the angling press and which has caught many trout for me while others have failed. It also takes trout on stillwaters where there is a hatch of mayfly. The body is black floss silk ribbed with oval tinsel or silver wire and is palmered with a badger hackle. The tail is three fibres from a cock pheasant centre tail, and the wing is formed by spinning a guineafowl or teal feather immediately behind the head, which is varnished black. The fly floats in the surface film and demands regular false casting to keep it dry and floating, but it always works.

Iron Blue

This pattern has taken many trout for me, particularly in the early season just before the mayfly hatch begins.

The body is traditionally dressed with mole fur, but grey rabbit can be substituted. Three iron blue cock hackle fibres are tied in as the tail, and an iron blue hackle is spun to form the wings. It is an easy fly to tie and very successful.

Lunn's Particular

Another very good dry fly. The tail is made from four fibres from the hackle of a red cock feather, and the body is formed from the quill of the same feather, which has been stripped. The wings are blue dun cock hackle points tied flat, and the hackle is red, natural cock. This is very effective tied parachute-fashion.

Silver Sedge

This is a pattern originated by F.M. Halford. The body is white floss silk ribbed with flat silver tinsel and palmered with a ginger cock hackle. The wings are starling or similar and the front hackle is again ginger cock.

Houghton Ruby

Another very good chalkstream fly invented by W. Lunn, the water-keeper to the Houghton Club on the River Test.

The tail is three white cock hackle fibres, and the body was originally a Rhode Island Red feather stalk died red. Nowadays, felt tip pens can halve the time spent in fly-tying, provided the colour used is water-fast. The wings are made from two light blue dun hen tips tied flat on the back and the hackle is a bright red cock hackle.

Parachute Pale Watery

This pattern was designed first and foremost to be tied as a parachute fly, unlike most dry flies, which have to be adapted.

The tail consists of three light blue dun hackle fibres and the body is a natural quill from a peacock 'eye' feather, the wings are light starling or similar, tied 'spent' and the hackle is pale watery dun hackle.

Rough Olive

This pattern can be tied in a no-hackle version, which works very well indeed.

The tail is blue dun cock hackle fibres and the body is olive seal fur ribbed with fine gold tinsel. The hackle is olive badger cock hackles. When tying no-hackle versions of any fly it is best to use a feather such as heron which will provide coarse fibres. Experience will provide the correct permutation as long as the colour is correct.

These patterns represent just a small cross-section of the vast number of dry flies that can be used by the fisherman. However, I would heartily recommend everyone to try tying their own patterns as well as the proved and trusted ones that have evolved over many years of use.

As I have mentioned before, I prefer my flies to float in the surface film, and there are a few innovative ways of tying dry flies which prove to be rather difficult for all but the most experienced fly-dressers. These include the parachute-hackled dry fly and the no-hackled dry fly.

Originally the parachute-hackled fly was tied with difficulty around a stub of nylon monofilament attached to the hook shank, and some dressers still use this method. The idea of the parachute hackle is to spin the hackle on the same plane as the hook shank (rather than at right angles to it). This leaves the body of the fly free to rest on the water if desired rather than canting at an angle. This type of fly is much easier to tie on a Partridge Swedish Dry Fly hook. The front part of the shank is kinked so that the hackle can be tied around this. The fly fishes with the hookpoint up so that it does not intrude into the water, possibly drawing the trout's attention to it.

The other notable innovation, the no-hackle fly, is exactly what the name implies. The fly is finished with no hackle at all, simply a body, a tail if appropriate, and a pair of wings. This one can be very difficult indeed to tie so that it drifts correctly on the water. It has a tendency to cant onto its side, if poorly tied, because of the lack of legs, formed by a hackle, which ordinarily provide stability.

Almost any dry fly can be tied parachute-style and no-hackle style, and it can sometimes be very worthwhile tying a recognized pattern utilising one of the above methods.

The no-hackle pattern was actually devised by two Americans, Doug Swisher and Carl Richards,

who wanted to present a fly which looked natural from below to the trout. Their original flies were tied fantastically small – size 18 to 28 in fact! However, the fly does work in larger sizes. The easiest way to create stability, these gentlemen discovered, was to add a ball of the body dressing to the bend of the hook and on top of the shank. The addition of a couple of splayed-out feather fibres for tails acted as stabilizers, and the fly was complete. It sounded fairly easy when I first read of it in Joe Brooks's book, but it takes quite a while to achieve a degree of success. It is best used to imitate olives and other ephemerids that naturally sport a tail which can be incorporated in the dressing.

This is not a common way of dressing a dry fly in Britain, but it is effective and well worth the effort. The body material must be buoyant, so seal fur is ideal. The wings in the original dressings were feather fibres, which gets over the problem of trying to match slips of wings for upright dry flies.

As well as these two innovations, there is another which is more common but which many overlook, and that is the use of hair fibres for the tying of upright dry-fly wings. The wings are only needed to make the fly alight correctly on the water and present a silhouette to the trout, and hair wings are often admirably suited to this end. They are also well worth experimenting with.

I have already mentioned several dry flies in the stillwater section, and they are also appropriate for rivers and streams. I tend to reduce the size of flies for casting at river trout, and I feel this is good advice for everyone.

Stalking a trout on a small stream.

CONCLUSION

As I said at the beginning, I will be satisfied if I have helped any flyfisher to improve his fishing. What I have not tried to do is to be all things to all men. For example, I am not an expert entomologist or fly-tyer, and I have left the expansion of those subjects to my fellow authors.

The enjoyment of the sport is of prime importance, as is the fact that everyone should be able to continue to fish (and shoot and hunt) unhindered and unhampered by the efforts of a militant minority. I feel that this dream is perhaps more achievable if we can all identify with each other, which means that we should continue to treat flyfishing as the gentle art. To share an idea or a conquest or a yarn with another at the waterside, or in some comfortable hostelry, is almost as important an aspect of flyfishing as the fishing itself.

There is nothing more pleasing than the beaming smile of a youngster who has taken his first trout. My eight-year-old boy, Michael, recently spent a day with myself and some friends at a small stillwater. Michael was retrieving a cast for the first time, when I pointed out a rising fish. I would have taken the rod to cast for him but he would not let me, and the next instant he was into a respectable and very acrobatic trout. He hung on to his relatively long rod with both hands, and after quite a scrap he landed on attractive, well-mended rainbow trout of 3½ lb (1.5 kg).

The next occasion when he handled a trout, I had hooked a brown. I gave the rod to Michael immediately so that he could play the fish, which he did with the same grim determination and stamina as the first time. He eventually landed a brown trout of just under 4 lb. His first two trout were an admirable brace, albeit that they had come from different waters on separate occasions.

I thought that too much success too soon might take the gilt off the gingerbread for him, but not at all. He follows me to the water with as much enthusiasm as ever, and is content just to sit and watch. And he sits next to me at the vice, wide-eyed and inquisitive. I only hope that Michael and his generation can continue to enjoy fishing throughout their lives.

It is not always the size of the fish that matters, but the quality of the fishing and the occasion. I think that every trout I have ever caught occupies a part of my memory, some fish occupy larger parts than others. Even if I cannot recall the exact occasion, I can walk by a stretch of stream or stillwater, or motor to a particular spot, and recall that I took a fish here or from just over there. As long as we can all view our sport with affection and defend our rights with the same enthusiasm which we muster in its pursuit, then the future is assured.

APPENDICES

GLOSSARY

Abdomen The narrow, tapered section at the rear of a natural fly's body.

Acid water River or lake water which has an acid content. Waters of this kind usually derive from peaty moorland.

AFTM Association of Fishing Tackle Makers; AFTMA – American Fishing Tackle Manufacturers' Association.

Alkaline water This is water rich in calcium, most commonly that of chalkstreams and limestone streams. Alkaline water is clear and generally rich in insects, crustaceans and molluscs, whose shells are strengthened by the calcium in the environment.

Back-cast The term used to describe the action of throwing the rod and line backwards, and allowing the line to unroll in the air, before making a forward cast.

Backing line Tough, rot-proof line made of Terylene (known in the USA as Dacron) or braided nylon (sometimes monofilament), which is joined to the flyline as a reserve for playing big fish. The backing line also serves to build up the level of the spool hub.

Beard hackle A bunch of fine fibres from the quill of a chicken's (or other bird's) neck feather, tied below the hook near the eye. Also known as throat hackle or false hackle.

Beat An area of waterside bank, on either a river or stillwater, allocated to one or more game fishermen for exclusive use over a fixed period of time.

Belly A curve in the line caused by the current on a river moving the line downstream ahead of the fly or bait, resulting in drag.

Bite The moment when the fish takes the bait. Bites are more often felt than seen.

Blowline A light fly line often made of silk, used for 'dapping' a fly on the surface of the water. A long rod and a breeze are needed to carry the line and fly far enough.

'Bob-fly The fly nearest the rod-tip or fly line when several are being used at once. It should 'bob' on the surface of the water.

Bow See 'Belly' above.

Breaking strain or BS The pounds test pull at which a line will break when it is dry.

Butt The thickest part of either a nylon leader or a feather or feather fibre used in flydressing. The term also describes the part of the rod held by the hand.

Buzzer The colloquial term applied to the *Chronomid* flies, midges and gnats which hover above the surface of all waters.

Caddis The larva of the sedge-fly. Also, the American word for sedge flies.

Caenis The scientific name for the Broadwing fly, a tiny, pale green insect which hatches in large numbers on summer evenings beside rivers and lakes.

Cannibal A large trout which has taken to eating other fish, including smaller members of its own species.

Casting The action of compressing the rod and projecting the fly line.

Colour When water is tinted with mud or peat, usually during or after heavy rainfall, it is said to be coloured.

Corixa The name used to describe the lesser water-boatman beetle, and the artificial fly which imitates it.

Cove knot Named after the well-known British stillwater flyfisher, Arthur Cove, this knot is used to join lengths of nylon in a leader, and to form strong droppers. It is also known as the four-turn water knot.

Cover This term describes the action of casting the fly to a fish or into a promising-looking area of water.

Cranefly More commonly known by the broad term of 'daddy-long-legs', over 250 different species of cranefly populate all kinds of waters. They are taken from the surface by trout and other fish.

Dangle When a fly has swung around in the current and is directly downstream of the rod it is said to be 'on the dangle'.

Dapping The art of playing a natural or artificial lure in such a way as to make it look as though it has fallen to the water from the branches of bankside trees or other natural obstacles.

Delivery An alternative term to 'covering' (see above).

Dibble The art of attracting fish by skimming and bouncing a wet-fly leader or bushy dry fly across the surface of the water.

Dorsal The main back fin of a fish.

Double taper A line with a tapering section at either or both ends of a swollen middle.

Drag The action by which the current forms a bow or belly in the line when the fly moves either faster than the current speed or across the current. The term also applies to the braking mechanism on a reel.

Drift A disturbance of the surface of stillwater, caused by wind or changing water temperatures bringing about a turnover of water.

Dropper A hook link of nylon attached to the main line.

Dry fly An artificial fly designed to float on the surface.

False casting A forward casting action used to gauge the ideal distance of the real cast, to dry a fly, or to increase the speed of a line.

Figure-eight Used to describe the way in which fly-line is gathered into the free hand when fishing the fly. The line is coiled into figures-of-eight around the fingers and thumb.

Fish 'Fishing the fly' means to let a river's current carry it after the cast, or to recover the fly by taking in line.

Floss A twisted silk or man-made fibre cord used as the body of many kinds of artificial flies.

Flotant A preparation applied to dry flies and some lines to make them float high on the surface of the water.

Fly A loose term used to describe most lures presented on a fly line and rod.

Fly line A line which has either weight to sink it, or buoyant material to make it float, coated onto it.

Forward taper A fly-line which has a tapered section towards the fly.

Foul-hook Hooking a fish anywhere other than in its mouth is known as a 'foul-hook'.

Four-turn water knot See 'Cove knot' above.

Fry The very young fish of most species.

Glide The name given to smooth, fast-flowing water being sucked out of a pool on a river by the mass of water moving downstream.

Grinner A type of knot used for tying flies to nylon monofilament leader. Much stronger than other knots used for this purpose.

Hackles Long feathers from the necks of chickens and cockerels, used to represent wings on flies.

Hatch The time when a large number of nymphs or pupas become fully-winged flies, often producing frantic feeding activity among the trout.

Imitative fly A fly which is manufactured to resemble as closely as possible the natural insect, crustacean or fish which is being reproduced.

Knotless tapered leader A cast of nylon tapered from butt to point and attached to the line without knots.

Lateral line The lines along the sides of a fish which contain its sensory organs.

Leader The length of nylon which connects the fly to the fly-line.

Leaded fly A weighted fly which will sink quickly to a good depth.

Lie A known resting place of fish. Fishermen jealously guard the knowledge of a lie!

Mayfly The largest of the upwing flies. Trout feed on them voraciously. In the USA, all upwing flies are referred to as mayfly.

Mend The term used to describe throwing a loop of line upstream to sink a fly down in the water and avoid drag.

Monofilament A single strand of line, usually nylon, most often used to make leaders.

Nymph A larva of the *Ephemeridae* family of flies or a fisherman's artificial representation.

Nymphing Fishing with an artificial nymph.

Pattern The fixed design of material and the position of parts which make up an artificial fly.

Point The finely tapered end-section of a fly cast, or the fly at the tip of the fly cast.

Pupa The stage following the larva in the life-cycle of some insects.

Recover To retrieve the line by pulling it in, by one means or another.

Retrieve The same meaning as recover.

Rise The action of a fish taking a fly, whether it be natural or artificial, when it is near the surface. A rise usually involves the breaking of the surface to form a ring in the water.

Roll-cast A method of casting the fly from the side, when there is no room for a back-cast.

Run When a hooked fish swims away at speed it is known as a 'run'.

Sedges Waterside plants or flies which belong to the *Trichoptera* order.

Shooting line The thinner line which extends behind the head or belly of a weight-forward line, and the thin braided or monofilament line behind a shooting-taper line. The action of letting such a line go in casting is known by the same term.

Spinner The final, winged stage in the life of an upwing fly.

Streamer flies Large artificial flies which are often used to represent small fish.

Stock fish Trout which are reared in captivity and stocked into fisheries are known as 'stock fish'.

Strip The term used to describe taking in the line by hand, as opposed to reeling it in.

Sunk line A fly-line that is fished well below the surface and often very close to the river or lake bed.

Tag A short, thick tail on an artificial fly, generally made out of silk or coloured filaments of nylon.

Takes A 'take' is a bite; the fish 'takes' the fly.

Tighten The act of raising the rod tip quickly to straighten the line and apply tension to it, in order to sink the hook into the mouth of a taking fish.

Tippet The fine tip of a leader, often knotted on and replaced as it shortens, in order to save the knotless taper.

Traditional flies Winged wet flies such as Peter Ross, Invicta and Mallard, often used for stillwater trout fishing.

Troll The term used to describe the action of towing a lure or fly behind a boat.

Upwing flies The *Ephemeroptera* order of flies, whose wings are nearly vertical and who possess two or three tails or *setae*.

Upwind Into the wind.

Wet fly An artificial fly used to fish below the surface, with either wings and a hackle or just a hackle.

Windward The direction from which the wind is blowing.

KNOTS

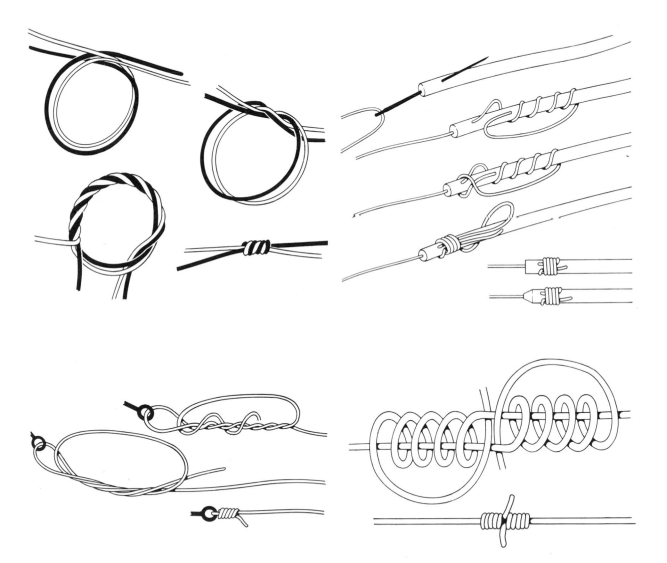

COVE OR FOUR-TURN WATER KNOT (top)
This knot is used for joining two lengths of light nylon of similar thickness; for instance, for adding a tippet to a leader.

GRINNER KNOT (above)
This is used for attaching flies to tippets.

NAIL KNOT (top)
This is used for attaching a leader, or a backing line, to fly line.

BLOOD KNOT (above)
This knot, also, can be used for attaching two lengths of nylon of similar thickness.

183

BIBLIOGRAPHY

Andrews, *Basic Fly-Tying*, Stanley Paul

Brooks, Joe, *Trout Fishing*, Harper & Row

Calver, J., *Bank Fishing for Reservoir Trout*, A. & C. Black

Bob Church's Guide to Trout Flies, Crowood Press

Church, Bob, *Reservoir Trout Fishing*, A. & C. Black

Church, Bob, and Gathercole Peter, *Imitations of the Trout's World*, Crowood Press

Clarke, Brian, *The Pursuit of Stillwater Trout*, A. & C. Black

Clarke, Brian and Goddard, John, *The Trout and the Fly*, Ernest Benn

Cockwill, Peter, *Big Trout Fishing*, Hamlyn

Collier, Dave, *Fly Dressing I*, David & Charles

Collier, Dave, *Fly Dressing II*, David & Charles

Fling, P., and Puterbaugh, D., *Basic Manual of Fly Fishing*, Sterling

Fling, P., and Puterbaugh, D., *Expert Fly-Tying*, Sterling

Goddard, John, *Super Flies of Stillwater*, A. & C. Black

Goddard, John, *Trout Flies of Stillwater*, A. & C. Black

Goddard, John, *Trout Fly Recognition*, A. & C. Black

Greenhalgh, Malcolm, *Lake, Loch and Reservoir Trout Fishing*, A. & C. Black

Greenhalgh, Malcolm, *Trout Fishing in Rivers*, Witherby

Ivens, T.C., *Stillwater Fly-Fishing*, Andre Deutsch

Lapsley, Peter, *Trout from Stillwaters*, A. & C. Black

Martin, Darrell, *Fly-Tying Methods*, David & Charles (Nick Lyons, USA)

McClane's Standard Fishing Encyclopaedia, Holt, Rinehardt & Wilson

Overfield, Donald, *50 Favourite Dry Flies*, A. & C. Black

Overfield, Donald, *50 Favourite Nymphs*, A. & C. Black

Overfield, Donald, *50 Favourite Wet Flies*, A. & C. Black

Parton, Steve, *Boat Fishing for Trout*, Allen & Unwin

Pawson, Tony, *Fly Fishing around the World*, Unwin Hyman

Pearson, Alan, *Catching Big Trout*, Stanley Paul

Pearson, Alan, *Introduction to Reservoir Trout Fishing*, Crowood Press

Price, Taff, *Fly Patterns – An International Guide*, Ward Lock

Taff Price's Stillwater Flies Book I, A. & C. Black

Taff Price's Stillwater Flies Book II, A. & C. Black

Taff Price's Stillwater Flies Book III, A. & C. Black

Veniard, John, *Fly Dressing Materials*, A. & C. Black

Veniard, John, *Further Guide to Fly Dressing*, A. & C. Black

Veniard, John, *Reservoir and Lake Flies*, A. & C. Black

Voss Bark, Conrad, *Encyclopaedia of Fly Fishing*, Batsford

Wakeford, Jacqueline, *Flytying Techniques*, A. & C. Black

Whieldon Tony, *Fly Fishing for Trout*, Ward Lock

Whieldon Tony, *Fly Tying*, Ward Lock

Whieldon Tony, *Stillwater Trout Fishing*, Ward Lock

Wilson, Dermot, *Fishing the Dry Fly*, Unwin Hyman

INDEX

PHOTOGRAPHY ACKNOWLEDGEMENTS

The author and publishers would like to thank the following for kindly supplying photographs for the book.

Colour: Bob Church page 86 lower; John Darling page 66; Chris Fairclough page 79; Peter Gathercole pages 12, 15, 38, 39, 51, 54, 63, 67 top and lower, 71, 74, 75, 78, 91 top and lower, 94, 95, 98–9, 103, 107, 111, 115, 119, 138, 139 top and lower, 143 top and lower, 147 lower, 151, 155, 163, 167, 171; David Grewcock pages 55, 130, 159; The Photo Source pages 22–3, 150; Graeme Pullen pages 14, 31, 34, 142; Roy Westwood page 59 top; Dermot Wilson pages 131, 134–5, 135 top right, 147 top. The photographs on pages 27, 43, 47, 59 lower, 83 top and lower, 86 top, were supplied by the author.

Black and White: Peter Gathercole.